The Myth of Nzala Mpânda

The imminence of the advent of the solar thought

By

Kiatezua Lubanzadio Luyaluka, Ph.D. (hon.)

Realized by the Editions Ntangu-i-Fueni
Kinshasa 2014

CONTENT

1   NTRODUCTION

The knowledge of one's past is a very valuable tool; it helps us to understand where we come from and also to prepare ourselves to better face the future. One of the essential elements of the past of the Black African is the history of his spirituality. But the study of the Black-African spirituality is not complete without an explanation of the place of fetishism. For the little word "fetish", brought to Africa by Portuguese traders, is now wrongly considered by many researchers as the essential qualifier of the worship by Africans to their God.[1]

In this book, explaining the difference between the notion of *n'kisi* and that of fetish, I show the genesis of human and demonic *min'kisi*[2], that I call fetishes, and I support my point with an ethno-linguistic interpretation of the myth of Nzala Mpânda.

This myth, left to the Kongo nation by initiated ancestors, is an oral will to allow the Black African to know the purpose of the introduction of fetishes and their destiny, but also to help him understand the imminent destiny of his civilization which is called to take back its place as the standard bearer of science and technology.

This myth is thus a teaching of immense importance because it predicts the current straying of the Black-African society, and its glorious destiny which is written as the abandonment of fetishes for the anchoring of thought in the high spirituality that made the glory of his ancestors since the memorable days of ancient Egypt, for a comeback of solar thinking, the thinking dear to the Black African.

---

[1] One can read for example Erwan Dianteil, « Kongo à cuba transformations d'une religion africaine », in *Archives de Sciences sociales des religions*, 2002, (janvier-mars) pp. 59-80. In his paper the author speaks of the influence of the Kongo religion on the cult of Cuban cult of Palo Monte; however, he shows the Kongo religion as being essentially the use of fetishes.

[2] Plural of *n'kisi*.

2 THE CONCEPT OF N'KISI

In my book *Vaincre la sorcellerie en Afrique*[3], I showed that a demonization campaign marked the emergence of Western man in the daily life of the Black African. This campaign, due to ignorance and prejudice, has resulted in the assimilation of the African notion of mystery (the initiatory teaching and the power it confers) to witchcraft. And this false assumption has ever since been the driving pattern of any research on witchcraft in Africa.

My research has elucidated the difference between the notion of the African initiatory mystery (called *kindoki* by the Besikôngo[4]) which is a knowledge that gives a power necessary for the progress of society, and the witchcraft which, in reality, is only the negative use of power and/or knowledge for the sole purpose of stealing, destroying, or killing.

The demonization of the notion of *kindoki* the Black African mystery, had as a major adverse conséquence, the demonization of all concepts that are satellites of *kindoki*, the initiatory mystery. Thus the notion of *n'kisi*, falsely translated by fetish since the arrival of the Portuguese in Africa, was also totally demonized. It is therefore imperative to revisit this concept in the light of the deep Black African culture.

---

[3] Kiatezua Lubanzadio Luyaluka, *Vaincre la sorcellerie en Afrique*, Paris : l'Harmattan, 2009.

[4] The people of the ethnics of the old Kingdom of Knngo, the people who designate the God Most-high by the term Nzâmbi Ampungu, or Nzâmi Mpûngu.

Thus, in the aforementioned book, I showed that *n'kisi* in its pure essence means a power, an awaked spiritual or ethereal sense or the assistance of spiritual being. The *n'kisi* may have a material symbol, physical or ethereal, and this symbol is also called *n'kisi*.

It should be noted that in the Kongo terminology the spiritual power is the power of God called Mpêve y'anlôngo (Holy Spirit) or the power of the *bisîmbi* (spiritual beings, angels). The *bisîmbi* can be good, i.e., imbued with divine power, or bad, i.e. driven by the devil (*nkadi ampemba*).

We know for example that the term *anlôngo* refers to what is holy or sacred.[5] The twins are seen in the Kongo nation as *bana b'anlôngo* (holy or sacred children). But these children come, according to Besikôngo, from *nkita* (the *n'kisi* of water)[6]. And the twins, who are born with an ethereal power according to the belief of the Besikôngo, derive their innate power from the good *bisîmbi* of water (though they do not always maintain the purity of this power in growing) their spiritual power (*n'kisi*) is therefore sacred and holy.

A Kongo proverb says: "*N'kêmbo an'kisi Nganga kimôya.*" (We enjoy the power of a *nganga*, a priest or an expert, only when he is alive with us, or when we

---

[5]At the birth of the twins the following song was used :
> *Eh Nsimba Ye Nzuzi eh ;*
> *Bana ban'longo (sacred children) ;*
> *Ehe, Ehe.*
Nsimba is the firs-born of the twin and Nzuzi is the next-born.
[6] According to the Kikongo-French dictionary of Karl Laman.

have faith that he is alive in the beyond.) This proverb was used by the initiates of Kimpasi[7] to refer to their spiritual power. It shows that the term *n'kisi* do not always refer to something demonic.

Another argument, which goes in the direction of the assertion that the term *n'kisi* means essentially power and that this one is not necessarily pejorative or evil, is that the word *mpûngu* a synonymous of *n'kisi* remained linked to the name of God in the expression Nzambi Ampûngu to designate the omnipotence of the Supreme Being. This expression, adopted by the Christian Church to this day in its translations of the Bible, shows that the words *mpûngu* and *n'kisi* can take even a divine connotation and can also be used in connection with the power of the Most-high.

In an anthropological perception, I can cite Hutton Webster who says in his book *la Magie dans les sociétés primitives*: "The Bantu speaking tribes of the Lower Congo have a term nkissi (*nkici*) which means rigorously the spirit, the power, the mystery "contained in medicines, trees, herbs, earth. From there it came to mean any mysterious power.""[8] It is clear here that the notion of *n'kisi* is defined as being essentially related to a spiritual power.

There are also etymological arguments. In his book *Voici les Jagas*, R. Batshikama wrote: "The word *n'kisi*

---

[7] One of the Kongo initiatory academies, the other being: the Lemba and the Kinkimba.

[8] Webster, H., *la Magie dans les sociétés primitives*, Paris : Payot, 1952, p. 29.

derives from the verb *kisika, strengthen* [the emphasis is mine], consecrate, sanctify, instruct, bless; synonymous *KINIKA, KISULA;* the contrary, is profane, insulting, to remove the blessings, synonymous *SINUKA*"[9] We clearly see here that the concept of n'kisi refers to power as I argued above, and it also includes a sacred connotation. For Batshikama *n'kisi* means religion and all terms related to *n'kisi* relate to religion. We are here, as we see, far from the essentially negative connotation attributed falsely to the Kongo concept by ignorance and prejudice to give it an inherently evil meaning.

About this assertion of Batshikama, it is worthy also to note that for Professor Margaret Washington[10], the Bakongo in pre-colonial times called the Christian church "*nzo n'kisi*" while the Christian Scriptures were for them "*min'kânda mian'kisi*". However, I am not of the opinion of Professor Washington when she affirms that the use of these terms was negative. I rather think that this practice arose from the deep understanding by the Bakongo that the divine power is the highest *min'kisi* and the church and the Bible being part of the sacred could only be related to *n'kisi*; in other words, the notion of divine *n'kisi* being the essence of their religion, the Bakongo could not see any other religion only in the guise of this deep conviction.

---

[9] Batshikama ba Mampuya ma Ndwâla, R., *Voici les Jagas*, Kinshasa, 1971, p. 188.

[10] Margaret Washington, *Le Legs universel de Kimpa Vita aux peuples noirs*, http /pbs.org/wgbh/aia/part1/1i3077.

In his book, which I alluded to above, Batshikama quotes Father Georges Gheel who gives in the first Bantu dictionary the following meanings for the word *wun'kisi*, an archaic form of the word *n'kisi*: holiness, divinity, divine will. In these senses we see that the word *n'kisi* refers to divine spiritual power and there is no reference whatsoever to the negative connotation that is attached now to this noble Kongo concept.

In his book titled *la Problématique crocodilienne à Luozi*, Professor Kimpianga Mahaniah makes a singular reference to *n'kisi* by stressing: "(...) In the pre-colonial society, people bought or learned from the owner of a *n'kisi* the powers necessary for the development of a productive activity to strengthen or increase the life force or for the acquisition of much prestige and strength to influence the invisible world, to commune with the spirits to dominate and govern, to become a healer and to be able to take revenge against his enemies or to master them to throw the bad luck to others, to protect oneself against witches."[11] This quote suggests that for Kimpianga *n'kisi* implies a power that can be used for the progress of society, i.e., a positive force.

The *n'kisi*, as an assistance of spirits, was and still is one of the ways to access to the *kindoki*, to develop ethereal faculties. However, among the Bakongo, the modes of initiation into the mystery include: the divine, the human and the demonic. Thus the *n'kisi* includes also: the divine, the human and the demonic aspects.

---

[11] Kimpianga Mahaniah, la Problématique crocodilienne à Luozi, p. 30.

2.1 Classification of *min'kisi*

The Black African initiatory mystery can be classified into three categories:

- The divine mystery
- The human mystery
- The demonic mystery

In the divine mystery the power is acquired by the purification of thought and the observance of spiritual laws. This power can be used only for good purposes. The divine mystery is the most powerful of the three aforementioned mysteries.

The human mystery includes all the mysteries where power is acquired by human means and therefore can be used for good or evil. The human mystery is that of the majority in all Black African society.

As for the demonic mystery, this is the one whose power is acquired by evil means: corruption of thought, demonic possession, human sacrifice, etc. If the divine and human mystery always had both formal education settings among Black Africans, the demonic mystery has never had it; since it is a deviation that was condemned by the society.

Since the presence of the traditional power in the Black-African society can be classified as divine, human or demonic, it goes without saying that the n'kisi, as essential to the devotion, must be classified as divine, human or demonic.

2.2 The divine n'*kisi*

The divine *n'kisi* is the spiritual power acquired by the purification of thought. As the emanation of divine power, this *n'kisi* is first God Himself (Mpûngu Tulêndo, the *n'kisi* which includes all authority)[12]. Being God Himself, this *n'kisi* had no material representation, because God is an absolutely spiritual Being, He is Spirit. So He can not be represented by something inferior. Van Wing writes about the Bakongo: "They have hundreds of fetish statues, representing men, animals, spirits; but none represents Nzâmbi. Those who spoke of fetish Nzâmbi among our Bakongo, dreamed or were victims of a misunderstanding. Nzâmbi is not of the category of beings that one can represent, of which we have and experimental knowledge."[13]

The divine *n'kisi* is not therefore the work of the expertise of a human hand. Acquired by man, it is only the manifestation of the immanent divine power by the Son of God, Mahungu; because every man is potentially a Mahungu, the man in the image of God, complete and having full dominion over all the earth. But the manifestation of the divine nature, the Kimahûngu, must be awakened by the initiation and implementation of the daily sanctification of thinking. The divine *n'kisi* is therefore the expression of the Kimahûngu, a notion

---

[12] This notion is found in Benin where a literal translation leads to the designation of God by the expression "Great Fetish". See Dumont, J., *L'histoire générale de l'Afrique*, Paris, 1972, p. 182.
[13] Van Wing, J., *Etudes Bakongo*, Léopoldville, 1938, p. 305.

equivalent to that of the Word, or the Christ, the perfect manifestation of God in the Christian tradition.

2.3   The human *n'kisi*

The main characteristic of the human *n'kisi* is that it is ambivalent: it can be used for good or evil purpose. Van Wing shows for example that the *n'kisi nkosi* is a fetish used to punish the marauders, it is also used to cure the disease that strikes a person when a parent stole in a farm belonging to others.[14] Thus the human *n'kisi* can both cause and destroy evil.

Bahelele says that after his initiation into Kinkîmba or Kimpasi, each student could learn a fetish, but not necessarily.[15] However, the same author states that "the student of Kinkîmba is a sacred being,"[16] implying that the *n'kisi* which he acquires, in addition to his divine initiation, is not an evil one, but a human power useful for the palliative protection of humanity.

2.4   The demonic *n'kisi*

In contrast to the divine *n'kisi*, its opposite, the demonic *n'kisi* involves the exercise of the power of evil spirits. Such power had no formal educational settings among the Bakongo. It must therefore be seen as a perversion of the human *n'kisi*, perversion condemned by society. I showed above that the human *n'kisi* could

---

[14] Van Wing, ibidem, p. 396.

[15] Bahelele Ndimisa, *Lusansu ye fu bia nkongo*, Kinshasa : CEDI, 1977, p. 50.

[16] Bahelele, ibidem, p. 49.

be ambivalent, so this *n'kisi* could be perverted and become demonic.

2.5   The concept of fetish

The term fetish comes from the Portuguese word *feitiço*. Hegba explains: "*Feitiço* itself is derived from the Latin *factitium*, artifact, artificial."[17] Speaking of the origin of this term, Van Wing says: "This name was applied by the discoverers of the 15th century to the statuettes and similar objects they saw in the hands of Blacks, in huts, and at intersections, objects of some rituals qualified as superstitious."[18]

The term fetish is unfortunately attributed wrongly to every *n'kisi* among the Bakongo, as among other Africans, by those who do not discern the link between the concept of divinity and the *n'kisi* among Black Africans. And even though they discerned, some went so far as to call God the "Great Fetish."[19]

The term fetish, per se, rather indicates something artificial, manufactured by the human hand. It is obvious that such a term should not be applied to divine *n'kisi*, insofar as it first means God himself (Mpûngu Tulêndo) and it refers also to the manifestation of His power, the

---

[17] Hebga, M., P., *Sorcellerie, chimère dangereuse…?,* Abidjan : INADES Editions, 1979, p.17.

[18] Van Wing, ibidem, p. 381.

[19] This concept is found also in Benin where a literal translation designates God the Most-high by the expression the "Great fetish". Confer: Dumont, J., *L'histoire générale de l'Afrique*, Paris, 1972, p. 182. I think that the original Benin expression must be a synonymous of *Nzâmbi Ampungu Tulendo.*

Word, the Kimahûngu. As I said above, van Wing shows that the Bakongo represented everything included in the vegetal world and in the animal one, yet God was never represented by the Black Africans, because He is transcendent Spirit. In the deep conception of the Bakongo, the divine *n'kisi* is therefore not a fetish.

Thus, the notion of fetish can apply only to that which is the work of the human expertise: the human *n'kisi*; just as it can apply to its perversion which is the demonic *n'kisi*. Moreover these are the only two *min'kisi* for which the Bakongo shape representations.

It is in the sense of human and demonic *n'kisi* that, for the need of the book, I will use the term fetish. For this use of the word fetish fits very well with the artificial connotation involved in this term in its original Portuguese meaning.

I also lean in the direction of the understanding of ancient Besikôngo for whom the effigies of churches, the crucifix, the rosary, etc., as receptacles of power, are merely fetishes: inventions of the human spirit.[20]

3   THE ORIGIN OF FETISHES

The hypothesis that I present in this chapter is that the use of fetishes among the Black Africans, is originally a human invention designed to perpetuate by human means (faith in matter and in the ancestors) the

---

[20] Margaret Washington, *Le Legs universel de Kimpa Vita aux peuples noirs*, http /pbs.org/wgbh/aia/part1/1i3077.

power acquired through the divine mystery, the divine *n'kisi*; fetishes are a palliative means for humanly perpetuating the power acquired through the divine initiation. I will present here a fiction that will serve as an illustration to show how a fetish could be created by an initiate of the divine mystery.

The old man Tuku is from the village Kûmbi; a village swarming with people and perched on a hill in the vicinity of the area of cataracts. Life in the country is peaceful, as can be seen on days when the market is held, days which are like festivities opportunities; because if the market is supposed to be a place where people come to sell or buy goods and services, the market of Kûmbi (named Nkênge-Kûmbi since it opens only the Nkênge day[21]), like all Kongo markets, is primarily a place of encounter with distant relatives or the place par excellence of enjoyment for the people of the country.

Tuku was born during the peanuts harvest; of course this is a really vague way to fix the date of an event, but it is the only one found by the ordinary mortals among the mothers in this region of cataracts, to reminisce all the events of the past of their families.

The village children are very active and docile. They start their day very early in the morning, to help their parents in the farm works, or to go about their own activities of small game hunting. But if Tuku during his youth was often deprived of the joy of participating in

---

[21] The Kongo week has four days: *nsona*, *nkênge*, *kându*, and *kônso*. Every clan has its day of rest.

these tasks, in fact it is due the fragile constitution of the child who often fell ill.

The people of Kûmbi, like all Africans, know no other cause of illness but witchcraft or disobedience against the laws of the ancestors. According to their deep conviction, man is born to live as long as possible on this earth; to die at young age is an anomaly for which palaver are needed to find the causes, always malefic, of death: a sorcerer must be criminalized.

To overcome Tuku's chronic diseases, diseases that the parents of the child had finally concluded as being due to *bankua n'soki*, the witches, Tuku was finally chosen to be part of an initiation of Kimpasi.

The Kimpasi is the greatest of the initiatory institutions of the Besikôngo. This University of the rainforest was intended to form traditional priests; so it was a sacerdotal initiation school, an academy of divine prophecy. The country had three initiatory institutions, the other two being the Kinkîmba and the Lemba. If the lessons of these last institutions were, like those of Kimpasi, also focused on the knowledge of God and the divinity of man, they do not yet have the priestly character. The Kinkîmba and the Lemba were therefore schools of little mystery, schools designed to create good living conditions in the country.

The Kinkîmba was a martial academy, which can be justified by the symbolism of the snake (python) that characterizes it; because the python (*mboma*) is the symbol par excellence of the martial power in Africa. As for the Academy Lemba, its preserve was the civil initiation; so it was the guarantor of all non-martial human knowledge, including the knowledge of the art of government and human healing.

The old Tuku was conspicuous by his wisdom; he never seemed to find problems resisting the penetration of his intuition. However, it was often necessary to express a lot of patience to finally have him deliver the solution to a problem against which all cogitations of the villagers ran aground: time never pressed him; the night is a good counselor, people affirm at Kûmbi.

If the old Tuku aroused the admiration of the whole village, he was at various points a great mystery for young people. For how this frail old and nonchalant man always managed to arrive ahead of them even though they preceded him in a long trip to go? How did he do to walk even faster than them, and that, whatever might be their vivid walking speeds? And even if they decided to run to finally arrive before the old initiated, they always found him ensconced at destination. And the worse of dishonor to their youthful pride is that he even blamed them for never hurrying like real young people must do! No a single young man of Kûmbi had really found an answer to the enigma of his rapidity.

All power in the divine mystery is the result of purification to being. Thus, Tuku's power of telekinesis is the result of a long practice of sanctification of his being mentally and through ablutions. The purpose of the initiation of Kimpasi is to allow the initiate to develop, by purification of his thought, the potential that is latent in every man. We are all born good, say the initiates of Kimpasi; at birth man has a perfect path well drawn before him, a path of prosperity. But the evil spirits always try to disorient him from his divine destiny. Thus, it is the objective of Kimpasi to enable mortal man to find the lost path that God had laid out for him.

Man in the Kimpasi, as in all Kongo initiatory academies, is actually a God who does not know it; in him abides the completeness of divinity. It is for this reason that every Muesikôngo calls his left part female and his right part male, this perfect nature of being is called the Kimahûngu. To become aware of the presence of the Kimahûngu and to live it in a life of holiness, a life of effective dominion over sin, is the key to success in all the mysteries of the Kongo initiatory schools. The Kimahûngu is thus the divine *n'kisi* par excellence. The man who is in possession of this powerful *n'kisi* is a Mahungu who knows it and who lives it.

Thanks to sanctification, the initiate of Kimpasi happens to live a perfect communion with the ancestors whose small voice he hears as clearly and distinctly as a very attentive ear hears in the savanna a call from a distant clearing. The ancestors walk with us through everyday life, they talk to us, but only the initiated ear can hear them; our weak faith prevents us to discern these distant channels yet still so close.

Lack of faith is the greatest handicap to the expression of the enormous potential of being that lie within each one of us. Tuku is fully aware of this truism. He also knows that by breaking the strength of unbelief, he may, by simple faith, even blind, pass in very short span of time the powers that only long years of patient, persevering and persistent practice off sanctification conferred him. So this is the way he finally chose to perpetuate in his extended family the power of telekinesis, of which he alone held the secret in the whole country of Kûmbi.

Among the Bakongo, man belongs to his mother's clan; the clan is matrilineal. It is useless to ask these Black Africans the reason for such a choice, the answer is always the same they provide as to the origins of their traditional values: it is the ancestors who taught us them. So it is to his nephew Lêmbamu, son of her younger sister, that Tuku decided to transmit his power of telekinesis, as it is supposed to be a heritage of the clan.

Lêmbamu was the most docile among the nephews of Tuku. Loving and helpful, the child loved to ask questions to the old Tuku, although sometimes they remained unanswered; the old African man is never in a hurry to communicate his wisdom to the youth. Do not conclude, however, that he is selfish; because what matters for the wise old African is not to stuff the head of the child with knowledge, but to help him become an adult, to push him to develop qualities that are essential to the development of intuitive skills: patience, perseverance, persistence, listening, intuition, wisdom ...

One day, while they were in the forest, Tuku promised Lêmbamu that he will reveal to him the secret of his power of telekinesis. The young man was ecstatic; he will be finally able to unravel the mystery of the speed of his old uncle. However some questions quickly broke into his mind; they often told him that the powers of Tuku were the result of an introduction to ancestral mysteries, and that this introduction into the world of the initiates involved previous difficult tests that really demanded bravery. Yet an introduction in due form to the great mystery of Kimpasi was not the approach taken by Tuku. The Old wanted something that could be perpetuated in the family from generation to generation without asking many binding efforts as he had to produce.

The ancestors can not transmit you their power if you do not strictly obey their laws, do you know it? Tuku asked to Lêmbamu.

Yes uncle; nodded the young man.

Tuku's lessons on the prescriptions and moral rules that should respect his nephew were often accompanied with the monotonous story of the genealogy of the family and how Tuku, through his exemplary conduct, had his training among Ancients. The young man often wondered why these same stories had been already recounted to him a dozens of times. However, he was careful not to be impertinent by daring to point out to Tuku that he already knew perfectly well that part of the tradition; there is maybe a wisdom to be learned, that has not yet been penetrated according to the estimation of the old wise of Kûmbi.

It was plausible that the young man was burning with impatience to receive the famous fetish of telekinesis whose existence his uncle had finally revealed to him; but he was careful not to display eagerness. What he did not suspect was that that fetish was an invention of his uncle, and that the old man was using in reality his prayer to work his exploits. His renowned power of Kimpasi was none other than the fruit of his acceptance of his nature of child of God, the Kimahûngu, and the daily sanctification of his thought. This power, he exercised only through the awareness of the presence in him of the sanctity of being, presence that allowed him to have access to the presence of the holy ancestors who surround him, so it was ultimately the spirit of saint-ancestors acting in him which enabled him to perform his prowess; his power of telekinesis was a divine *n'kisi*.

One day the old Tuku called Lêmbamu and spoke to him in these terms:

I'm happy with the way you respect the requirements bequeathed by our beloved ancestors. It is thus time for you to learn the power of telekinesis. Here! Take this fetish.

Tuku handed Lêmbamu a small gazelle skin bag containing miscellaneous objects which he alone held the mastery of composition.

Thanks uncle, threw the young man joyfully.

We are going to travel to a remote area using the power of the ancestors, remember well what I'll do and the formulas that I will voice.

Lêmbamu watched with a devotional attention everything that was done by Tuku. The Old, knowing that human power can easily be deflected and lend itself to a negative use, and despite all the precautions he had taken to avoid this unfortunate drift, added:

You must never use that power otherwise than for the purpose of doing good, if not, the ancestors will turn their backs to you and you will lose their assistance, he advised the young man firmly.

Tuku mumbled some formulas and asked Lêmbamu to hold him and close his eyes. When at last he was ordered to open his eyes, great was his surprise to find that they were already at destination. "This fetish is really effective, he thought silently." This instantaneous trip was only the first of a long series of exploits performed by Tuku with his nephew. The Old always took care to strike the imagination of Lêmbamu to inculcate the belief in the power of telekinesis fetish.

Thus, with repeated use, always with his uncle, the faith grew in Lêmbamu that the telekinesis fetish actually works. There remained to the Old only to order him to try it alone. With increased faith of the young man (that he did not even know yet), he could move by the sole use of the fetish: the power of telekinesis acquired by his uncle through the principles of the divine mystery came to be transmitted through a mere blind faith in the ancestors. And so a fetish was born.

Tuku's power of telekinesis is a divine *n'kisi* a power acquired through diligent practice of sanctification of being, while the power of telekinesis of Lêmbamu is a fetish, a human *n'kisi*, power which can be perpetuated by the simple faith in the ancestors through an object made by man. In addition, Tuku can only use his power for good purpose, while Lêmbamu can use his in good as in evil ways. However, this latter use is strictly forbidden him, unless the protection of individuals or the welfare of the community be the mobile.

This story thus illustrates how fetishes were created by initiates involved in the divine mystery. Fetishes are temporal means used by our ancestors to preserve the Besikôngo during the period of straying resembling to the sleep of a civilization. Several ethnographic elements can justify this assumption of the divine origin of *min'kisi*.

4 THREE MYSTERIES IN THE KINGDOM OF KONGO

I said in my illustration in the previous chapter that there are three kinds of mysteries among the Bakongo. It is important to clarify the concept of this initiatory trilogy for the understanding of the parallelism that I will further establish between the initiatory system of ancient Egypt and the Kongo system. I will in this chapter show more clearly the existence of three initiatory mysteries among the Besikôngo: the great mystery, the civil mystery and martial mystery.

The main Kongo initiatory schools are: the Kimpasi the Lemba and the Kinkimba. These Kongo initiatory schools sometimes had other names in other area of the kingdom, but whatever the label, each initiatory academy among the Besikôngo, as elsewhere in the Black Africa, took place in the context of one of the currents which I will describe in the following lines:

4.1   The three Kongo mysteries

The classification I will give here is one that is based on the professional classes. It is true that in terms of their nature, the initiatory knowledge and power can be grouped into:

- Divine Mystery, where the power acquired by the purification of thought can only be used in good ways.

- Human Mystery, where the power is acquired through human means and can be used for good or for evil ways.

- Demonic mystery, where power is acquired by evil means, and can only be used in evil ways.

But in terms of professional divisions the Kongo initiatory system rather obeys the following classification:

- The great mystery, or the priestly mystery,

- The little mystery, which in turn includes two branches:

- The martial mystery

- The civil mystery.

In practice there were more than three initiatory schools among the Beskôngo: however, I would hope that each Kongo initiatory Academy was part of one of the above three professional categories. This was consistent with the principle of trinity on which the Kongo nation was built.

4.1.1 The great mystery

The Kongo great mystery is represented by the Kimpasi; because the mystery of this school aimed essentially at the training of prophets. Thanks to its ritual purifications performed by using constant ablutions, the Kimpasi used to lead initiates to be able to hear the voices of saints and ancestors and finally to be able to see and talk with them as a man speaks to his fellow man. Thus among the offspring of the initiatory academy of Kmpasi are the great figures of the Kongo spirituality of our time: Kimpa Vita and Kimbangu. [22].

That the Kimpasi was a prophets training academy is also seen in the following fact: at the foundation of the Kongo Kingdom, King Lukeni, allied with the high priest Nsaku ne Vunda, however this last was of the region of the Bampângu, whose soil is the stronghold of the Kimpasi. Besides, the clan Nsaku (to which belonged the great priest) is considered in the Kongo tradition as "*N'singa wolo wakulumukina Nzambi Ampûngu.*" Batshikama explains this expression as follows: "The sacred golden cord by which descends God Almighty."[23] This implies that Nsaku and his descendants are the agents of the revelations coming from the Most High God through the holy ancestors, the clan Nsaku includes a line of prophets. It is always from this clan that came the high priests of the Kingdom of Kongo And therefore the school that reigned in the region of Bampangu could be only a training school of the prophets.

Etymologically, the word kimpasi comes from the term *mpasi* which, in the old Kikongo, means wealth[24].

---

[22] See in my book Vaincre la sorcellerie en Afrique, pp. 32-33.
[23] Batshikama, R., *Voici les Jagas*, Kinshasa, 1971, p. 181.

However, the Bakongo evolving in a solar culture, a culture centered on the divine, their great wealth can only be in reality spirituality. Thus Kimpasi is the school of the great spirituality. So it is the Kimpasi which is the guarantor of the formation of prophets in the Kongo milieu.

4.1.2 The civil mystery

The civil mystery by excellence in the Kingdom of Kongo is the Lemba. The Lemba is the initiatory school that dominated the northern part of the Kingdom of Kongo. Speaking of this school Janzen reveals the following descriptions: "It is described as having been "a medicine of the village"; "a medicine of the family and its perpetuation"; "fertility medicine"; "the sacred medicine of governing" (*Lemba i n'kisi wangyaadila*) according to one clan head; "the government of multiplication and reproduction" (*luyaalu lua niekisa*), by a former Lemba wife; and "sacred medicine integrating people, villages and markets" (*n'kisi wabundisa bantu, mavata ye mazandu*), by a contemporary merchant and clan head who wrote a local history."[25]

All these descriptions provided by people who inhabited the region which was dominated by the Lemba show that this academy was a school of civil mystery, i.e., a non-martial academy focused on human training to create conditions of peace and progress in Kongo society. To my mind, this is the way Janzen sees

---

[24] Le mot *mpasi* garde encore le sens de richesse dans le *tshiokwe*, l'un des dialectes *kôngo*, de la région de Bandundu.

[25] Janzen : *Lemba, 1650-1930*, New York : Garland Publishing inc., p. 4.

this initiatory academy when he says in his book *Lemba 1650-1930* that Lemba is a "major historic cult of healing, trade, and marriage relations,"[26]

Etymologically, the word *lemba* comes from the verb *lemba* meaning to soothe. The Lemba had therefore the task of pacifying the country soothing negative forces illness, crisis, tension, etc., between the Besikôngo.

4.1.3 The martial mystery

The martial initiation among the Bakongo was the preserve of the Kinkimba Academy. The mystery of the Kinkîmba reigned triumphantly on the west coast of the Kingdom of Kongo, from the territory of Bayombe (Democratic Republic of Congo) to Loango (Congo) through the Bawoyo at the mouth of the Congo River.

Etymologically, the word *kinkîmba* comes from the verb *kimba* means to run and it shows that this initiation was related to physical prowess. That the Kinkîmba was a military academy is seen in the symbolism of the snake attached to it. Among the Bawoyo at the end of his initiation, the disciple of the Kinkimba had to be licked by a live snake.

Mvog Ekang confirms that the serpent is the symbol of martial initiation among Africans, to the extent that he writes about the python in the So initiation among the Betis of Cameroon: "The rite of vine-python was a training endurance which is equivalent to the contemporary military training."[27]

---

[26] Janzen, Ibidem, p. 3.

[27] Mvog Ekang, *Cameroun – religion traditionnelle,*

The python (*mboma*) in Kinkîmba is the symbol of martial force of Tafu-maluangu (Mahungu), the man in whom abide the Kimahûngu, the completeness of God; completeness manifested by the presence in him of the male and female divine in nature. For this reason the python itself is represented in the sky by the rainbow. For this peaceful sign of the Most High God appears to us in the sky as a bright multicolored male arc in front of another female dim arc. Rainbow therefore manifests the power of the Word mastering, in heaven, the forces of nature for the protection of humanity.

About python (*mboma*) one must also remember that the great military commander was called in Kikongo *n'kuamboma*, which gives in Teke language: *ngamboma* the name of a great Teke military leader of Kinshasa.

The Prime Minister of the Kingdom of Loango was called Ma-Mboma-Tchiluangu. About the meaning of this term Joseph Kimfoko Mandoungou, the curator of the museum of Loango (museum located near the city of Pointe-Noire in Republic of Congo), explains that involves "the acquisition by the character of the Nthchiama (rainbow), the animal incarnation is the python (*mboma*), which extends its magical protection on all that surrounds it."[28] We see here clearly highlighted the idea of a defensive military fortification.

Speaking of the contents of the initiatory hut of the Kimkîmba, Bittremieux gives us the following

---

[28] Kimfoko Madoungou, J., *le Guide du musée*, Pointe-Noire, 1985.

information: "One saw also spread therein the usual instruments of the stronger sex: knives, creeper hoops, pebble gun, gourds for palm wine; then, wooden rifles for tournaments (...)"[29]

These "usual instruments of the stronger sex" do not they arise thought of a military training in good and due form, especially when we find that the guns were used in tournaments? The Stono Revolution[30] teaches us that the guns were part of the weapons used by the Kongo initiates trained in war in the province of Mbamba. The Kinkimba was therefore a military academy.

4.2 Survival of Kongo initiation

The Besikôngo initiatory system had trouble with the colonial enterprise from the beginning of the intrusion of the West in the lives of black Africans. Misunderstanding, prejudiced and malice led the missionaries and the Western seculars to work for the destruction of Kongo spiritual values; thus Kongo assets were unfortunately perceived by them as evil, even though in reality they were often kept as very precious valuables to cram their museums overseas.

However, it is also noteworthy that the Bakongo are among the few Africans who happened, despite the centuries of opposing thrust, to maintain the essential of

---

[29] Bittremieux, L., *la Société secrète des Bakhimba au Mayombe*, Bruxelles, 1936, p. 37.

[30] An uprising of the enslaved Bakongo in 1730 in South Carolina in USA, who under the leadership of Jemmy, fought victoriously against the Whites thanks to the riffles taken by breaking a arsenal and they went to Florida as tree men.

the initiatory teachings until the 1930s. Thus we can still find families where the quintessence of initiatory knowledge is still transmitted from parents to their offspring. This is especially true of Kimpasi which could well be reduced to its simplest expression, namely the sanctification of being.

Kongo nation is today in the sacred obligation to help the Black Africans to regain the ancestral pathway leading to the climax of the initiatory knowledge and power. It behooves therefore to the Besikôngo to give to their race siblings of Africa and the diaspora the sacred initiatory secret they have had the honor to keep for the prosperity of humanity in the third millennium.

5 EVIDENCE OF THE DIVINE ORIGIN OF FETISHES

I will develop in this chapter, based on ethnographic elements, the assumption that I mentioned at the end of the third chapter, the hypothesis that fetishes are rooted in the divine initiatory tradition, they are the original work of the initiates of the divine mystery, a human means of transmission and perpetuation of their power through faith in matter and the assistance of the ancestors. Among the ethnographic evidence are:

- The *ndumbululu* of the fetishes,
- The testimonies of the Bampângu,
- The myth of Nzala Mpânda.

5.1 The *ndumbululu* of the fetishes

The *ndumbululu* is a short epic poem that gives an overview of the history of a clan or a *n'kisi*. Each clan among the Bakongo has its *ndumbululu*. These poems, which are part of the clan badges of honor, are often in an archaic Kikongo, which shows that their origin dates back to very ancient times in Kongo dia Tuku, the original homeland of the Bakongo.

In his book *Etudes Bakongo*, van Wing talks about the fetishes, human or demonic *n'kisi*, used by Kongo ethnics of east. Among these fetishes is found the *n'kosi*. This fetish was used in the Bampângu[31] to protect their homes, fields or any other asset in tackling thieves and witches. Van Wing gives of the fetish *n'kosi* the following ndumbululu:

> *E n'kosi !*
> *Kimênga kiaku umwene kio,*
> *A nsidi sa,*
> *Zibula rnakutu.*
> *Nge N'kosi mbûngu zi mênga,*
> *Nge mûntu ye zi'na,*
> *Mpati aku mono,*
> *Ngang'aku mono.*
> *Utuka ku nani ?*
> *Utuka ku na Sâmba.*
> *Na Sâmba ukubakila ku ba mbuta zândi,*
> *Ba mbuta zândi bakutombula ku masa.*[32]

---

[31] Les Bakongo situés en amont du fleuve.
[32] Van Wing, J., *Etudes Bakongo*, Leopoldville, 1938, pp. 395-396

He provides of this *ndumbululu* of the fetish *n'kosi* the following translation:

> *Eh N'kosi!*
> *Your blood you saw and drank it,*
> *I'll tell you,*
> *Open your ears.*
> *You, N'kosi that sheds blood.*
> *You man with your name,*
> *Your landlord, it's me,*
> *Your nganga is me.*
> *For from whom do you come?*
> *You come of the Lord Samba.*
> *The Lord Samba took you from his Elders,*
> *His Elders brought you up from the water.*

This *ndumbululu* therefore shows clearly that the fetish *n'kosi* has been passed down from generation to generation until it fell into the hands of the Lord Samba. But, the first *n'kosi* the Elders took it out from water. Here we must understand that water in the Kongo spiritual tradition is the symbol of holiness; water implies the holy world of the illuminated ancestors. The first *n'kisi n'kosi* is the work of the ancestors engaged in the divine mysteries: it is a divine power transmitted by faith as temporal power fetish called *n'kosi*.

One can read the same thing about the fetish named *kapiângu* that the same author defines as follows: "This fetish or rather the spirit of this fetish, incorporated into a statue is universally feared. It is used to investigate and prosecute thieves and committers of witchcraft."[33]

Here is the ndumbululu of kapiângu as collected by van Wing among the Bampângu:

> *You, Kapiangu man with your name,*
> *I'm your owner,*
> *I am your master nganga.*
> *From whom do you come?*
> *You came from Na Lumba.*
> *Na Lumba received you from his elders.*
> *His Elders took you out of water.*[34]

The ndumbululu are unanimous and clear about the fetishes: the first *n'kisi* is divine, and his power is perpetuated from generation to generation in human form; fetishes are of divine origin.

5.2 Testimonies of the Bampângu

The evidences I collected from the Bampângu abound in the same direction, they show that the origin of the fetishes is in the divine mystery, a work of the ancestors engaged in divine initiation. According to one of my informants, the Elders in the village complained to the ancestors aside the rivers speaking in these terms: "Really in this whole hamlet you can not find anyone on whom you can bring up the *n'kisi* from water? "[35]

One ritual for obtaining this original *n'kisi* consisted in immersing the disciple in the water where he would

---

[33] Van Wing, *Etudes Bakongo*, Leopoldville, 1938, P. 388.

[34] Van Wing, ibidem, p. 391.

[35] Testimony taken from Kondo Makela who described to me in this way a scene constantly lived at the hamlet of Kimuanga sector Ngeba, in Kongo Central (DRC).

come up with the powers received from ancestors. The person thus initiated had powers beyond those of other initiates of the human mysteries.

5.3   The myth of Nzala Mpânda

I pointed out in my introduction that the ancestors have left us this myth to remind us of the origin and destiny of the human *n'kisi*, fetishes, among the Black Africans. The study of this myth will be the subject of the next chapter.

6   THE MYTH OF Nzala Mpânda

This Kongo myth is reported us by van Wing, a missionary of the Society of Jesus, who has long lived among the bampângu ethnics, Bakongo which are upstream of the Nzadi Kongo, the Congo River. This myth has been told by several Elders to Van Wing about the origin of fetishes. It reads:

"Nzala Mpânda came from heaven. Nzambi Mpungu dropped him down (*unsotwele*). He came to Kongo at Mpangu and Luango. In this village he worked a lot of wonders. He took a pestle and dived into the ground; the pestle began to grow and became a *mbota* (*Milletia versicolor*). In the morning he planted a banana, at noon a bunch grew; in the evening it was ripe. He wove a bag with pineapple fiber and put in it palm wine; not a single drop was lost. He took another bag, and filled it with sand, and the sand become salt. He crossed the Ngufu river, and set his foot on a rock (*tadi di nkwangila*). The imprint of his foot remained there. Before his death he gave to Mvumbi Mbumbulu very powerful *min'kisi*. After his death people, morning him, set the corpse tied with cloths against the wall of the hut. Yet here a Mbambi (antelope horn shaped fo whistling) whistled. Nzala Mpânda stands and rises. But soon he dies again. A pit is prepared and he is brought therein: as they want to drop him therein, he rises and ascends to heaven. After wards, the village elders, looking at the sky, there were a a path and then suddenly one of them rises and disappears with arms extended. Nzala Mpânda had come to take him. It was at the same time that there was a great eclipse of the sun, that day all was clear and then immediately all was dark, and no one left his house to go to the fields."[36]

6.1   Exegete of the myth of Nzala Mpânda

The two main characters of this myth are clearly identified as being named: Nzala Mpânda and Mvumbi Mbumbulu. However, for a clear understanding, it is important to dissect the deeper meaning of these two expressions. The Bakongo have a strong sense of what I call "crypto-semantics", i.e., a choice of words whose profound hidden meaning can be revealed only by a semantic analysis based on etymological origins of the expression. I am convinced that the names Nzala Mpânda and Mvumbi Mbumbulu do not designate human beings, as some believe, but rather states of the Black-African civilization, as I will demonstrate in the following lines.

---

[36] Van Wing, J., *Etudes Bakongo*, Leopoldville, 1938, pp. 418-419.

6.1.1 The meaning of Nzala Mpânda

The term *nzala* comes from the verb *zala* which means in Kikongo: to be filled. The substantive *nzala* coming from the verb *zala* mean: the fact of being filled; Bentley gives the following definition: "being full"[37] Therefore figuratively the term refers to a peak.

Mpânda comes from the verb *hânda* which in Kikongo means: to be initiated into the mystery or to the use of a fetish. *Mpânda* the substantive that follows takes the sense of: how to learn. Figuratively Mpânda mean knowledge and power gained through an initiation.

Thus, as I noted above, the term Nzala Mpânda do not refer to a historical human person, a Mwesikôngo who lived in the past, but rather it expresses the idea of the peak of knowledge and initiatory power among Black Africans.

6.1.2 Other interpretations of Nzala Mpânda

My interpretation of "Nzala Mpânda" is not the first attempt in history; others before me have had to think about the famous Kongo myth and gave interpretations that lean towards cosmogonical approaches.

6.1.2.1 Interpretation of Lusala lu Ne Nkuka

In his article titled *les Traces de Dieu dans les cultures*, Professor Lusala, who is the first to propose an

---

[37] «Nzala, 2, n., a being full. » Voir : Bentley, H., *Dictionary and grammar of the kôngo language.*

interpretation of the myth that is the subject of my study in this chapter says about the character of Nzala Mpânda: "The God-among-the-men called Osiris among the ancient Egyptians, Gueno among the Fulani, Obatala for the Yoruba, Kiranga or Ryangombe in the area of great lakes and Nzala Mpânda among the Bakongo."[38]

It is clear that my interpretation of the myth of Nzala Mpânda highlights a different meaning of the term than the one sustained by Professor Lusala. As for the Kongo vision of Christ, I demonstrated in my book *la Religion Kongo*[39] that the Christian concept of God among men is rather the equivalent to the Kongo notion of the Kimahûngu; and Osiris, the Son of God, is the equivalent in Kongo tradition to Mahungu, the man in whom is the Kimahûngu, the completeness of God in His image.

6.1.2.2 Interpretation of Nkusu Kiambu

Another attempt to interpret the term "Nzala Mpânda" is the one provided by Nkusu Kiambu, the Spiritual Chief of Vuvamu[40], during a TV show.[41] For Nkusu,

---

[38] Lusala lu Ne Nkuka, « les Traces de dieu dans les cultures » in *Congo nova*, http://www.congonova.org.

[39] Kiatezua Lubanzadio Luyaluka, *la Religion kôngo*, Paris : l'Harmattan, 2010.

[40] Vuvamu is a religious movement of consciousness awareness of the Black race, sustaining the return to the Black-African religion, as the only issue for the development of the Black man. This movement is based in Kinshasa.

[41] It was during the show "Identité particulière" of Joseph Kabongo of "Antenne A", a TV station of Kinshasa.

Nzala Mpânda is the first ancestor of the Kongo man; his name literally means "nail of the covenant" and refers to the sacred covenant between Nzâmbi Ampûngu and this original Mukongo.

This argument, of the Spiritual Leader of Vuvamu, do not resist ethno-linguistic analysis. Indeed, the nail is called in Kikongo: *luzala*. The plural of the term is *nzala*. Thus, following the idea of Nkusu the translation of this expression must rather be: "nails of the covenant." If Nkusu puts the term "nail" in the singular and consciously ignores the fact that *nzala* is plural, it is that he is aware of two elements:

- The nail in the modern Kikongo alludes figuratively to the signature.

- If there had been a covenant between God and man, the only signature that would have been is that of man, for God is a Spirit.

The literal translation "nails of alliance" implies that there were several signatures, that of man and that of a conclave of the gods maybe. This of course is an aberration; especially when one considers that it is not by a signature that Besikôngo were sealing their traditional alliances, but by weddings and gift exchanges. When Ne Lukeni, the founder of the kingdom of Kongo, made a covenant with Nsaku ne Vunda he married the niece of the latter. Moreover, the term Mpânda in Kikongo does not mean alliance, as I have shown above.

6.1.3 Partial Interpretations

In addition to what has been said above, the interpretation of Professor Lusala and the spiritual leader of Vuvamu are partial with respect to the myth; they give us an attempt to explain the term Nzala Mpânda but are silent on all other aspects of the myth: Mvumbi Mbumbulu, the eclipse, the *n'kisi*, the footprint of Nzala Mpânda, etc.

I am strengthened to conclude, therefore, that my interpretation is the only one so far which is complete and consistent with the ethno-linguistic analysis: The Nzala Mpânda does not refer to the Kongo cosmogony, neither to a human being; but to the climax of the initiatory power.

6.1.4 The meaning of Mvumbi Mbumbulu

The Kikongo word *mvûmbi* means human corpse. However, I think this is not the meaning mentioned in this myth, because giving a fetish to a corpse has no meaning; the corpse can not act, hence it can not use a fetish so powerful be it. So I think there is really a semantic confusion here; the denotation that must be used in the case of our myth is *m'vûmbi*. The confusion, in my opinion, can be explained in two ways: either the usage eventually substituted a meaning that was not appropriate, or even the author (van Wing) who do not use accents in writing Kikongo words, writes in the same way the two words which then become homonyms, and he creates thus a misunderstanding.

M'vûmbi refers to an intermittent rain that takes time to stop. The *m'vûmbi* can last several days and nights, a *muesikôngo* woman told me of a *m'vûmbi* she witnessed in her hamlet and which, according to her recollections, lasted about four consecutive days, crippling farm activities. The *m'vùmbi* therefore cause slowdown among the Bakongo. The term *m'vûmbi* in the myth of Nzala Mpânda therefore refers to a period of reduced initiatory activity, to a decrease of initiatory knowledge and power in black Africans.

The term mbûmbulu comes from the Kikongo verb *bumbula*. Defining this verb Bentley in his dictionary of Kongo writes: "to grope about (in the dark or as a blind man)."[42] This sense combines very well with that of *m'vûmbi* to mean: a long period of reduced active due to straying in darkness. And this is especially plausible when one learns that a "night" caused by an eclipse is part of our myth.

6.1.5 The meaning of the eclipse

One of the elements that are part of the scene described in the myth of Nzala Mpânda is an eclipse. This image refers to a passage from an epistemological base to another; the transition from the solar epistemology to the lunar one.

I show in my book *les Bases épistémologiques du savoir négro-africain* that Blacks and Whites do not use the same epistemological bases. There are two main approaches available to man for the acquisition of knowledge: the lunar approach and solar one.

In the lunar approach thought is focused on matter. This approach is based on human reason as an essential source of knowledge. The lunar approach

---

[42] See Bentley, H., *Appendix to dictionary and grammar of the kôngo language*. London, 1895.

rejects anything that is not based on rational reason as superstitious.

The solar approach is the approach par excellence of the Black African man. Its characteristic is a thought turned toward the heavens, toward the upper humanities; truth is perceived as essentially a revelation. Solar approach emphasizes the freedom of the soul; thus the oracles plays a big role in this approach unlike in the lunar approach.

The lunar eclipse symbolizes the temporary supremacy of the lunar approach over the solar approach which is more effective and is more appropriate to the Black African. This eclipse implies a temporary darkening of the consciousness of the Black African, darkening which implies a reduced activity of his initiatory knowledge and power due to the adoption of paradigms that are foreign and inappropriate to the deep tradition of the Black man.

6.2   Explanation of the myth

The myth of Nzala Mpânda is an explanation of the origin of fetishes as human *n'kisi*. The myth tells us first that the peak of initiatory knowledge and power among the Black Africans, personified in the myth as the Nzala Mpânda, was the result of divine grace given to their ancestors. Because, it is God who sent down the Nzala Mpânda on earth: "Nzala Mpânda came from heaven. Nzâmbi Ampûngu dropped him."

Thus, through their initiatory system that puts God at the center of everything, in agreement to the solar thought, our ancestors have achieved a high level of knowledge and power. Once at the peak, they have made many technological prowesses. These feats are symbolized in the myth by the fact that Nzala Mpânda "took a pestle and dived into the ground; the pestle began to grow and became a *mbota* (*Milletia versicolor*). In the morning he planted a banana, at noon a bunch grew; in the evening it was ripe. He wove a bag with pineapple fiber and put in it palm wine; not a single drop was lost."

All these feats seem miraculous and outside of the scope of the application of science for the lunar thought. But it must be remembered that the Black man hitherto still evolved spiritually and scientifically in his epistemology, which is solar in nature. These exploits are consistent with a technology based on a system of thinking where religion and science put God at the center of their activities, a more efficient technology, although it uses less matter.

The myth also tells us that the exploits of the ancestors have left indelible marks because Nzala Mpânda "set his foot on a rock (*tadi di nkwangila*). The imprint of his foot remained there." This footprint is intended to serve as testimony to future generations, and certainly it also serves to push them into the path of the high spirituality on which are based the exploits Nzala Mpânda. But the imprint was also left in order to instill in these generations the need to excel, to break the current stalemate of their civilization.

The civilizations are like mortal men; after intense exercise of their physical activities men must rest to renew their power, civilizations also disappear or they go through a hibernation that allows them to rebuild their forces in order to resume their intense activity later. Ancient Black Africans therefore knew that their civilization was going through this time of cultural hibernation, the final phase of which is symbolized in the myth by the night that comes from the eclipse.

But contrary to the expectations of people, Nzala Mpânda, the arrival of the peak of the prowesses of the solar thought, was not an event without having no future, those who thought him dead were indeed wrong in their speculation; because soon, says the myth, Nzala Mpânda revived again for a short period of time.

6.3   Nzala Mpânda throughout the history

The myth of Nzala Mpânda teaches us that there were two climaxes of initiatory knowledge and power among Black Africans: the great and the small. The question is therefore the place of these two advents in time. Van Wing assists us in this process when he shows the existence of similar myths among other Black African peoples then the Bakongo; we can read in his book on this subject:

"Torrend collected such a legend among the Batonga. This Mpande is a Son of God. He lives in the airs, in the rainbow. He once took Monze, when he was still a baby. He made him fly and stay in the air. After he brought him down, he fell with a noise *po*! And said: "I bring the rain", etc..

"Father Casset in his turn noted a variation[43] of the same legend: "A Monze, they say, was transported to heaven after his death, leaving his footprints on a rock near the Magoye River. But this imprint is not visible at all. The spirit of this Monze passed to another, who inherited the power to cause rain."" [44]

These myths recounted by Torrend and Cassette were collected from the Tonga (or Batonga), peoples of Southern Africa. The Batonga form one of the largest ethnic groups in southern Zambia. They are also found in Zimbabwe and Malawi.

The existence of similar myths among other Black African peoples is evidence that the advents of the peak of the solar thinking, that the myth Nzala Mpânda alludes to, took place before the establishment of the Kingdom of Kongo. This then leads me to the following hypothesis: considering the hypothesis of the Bantu migration from the east to southern Africa and their progress northward to the Congo Basin by the west coast, the first coming of the Nzala Mpânda (the peak of the Black African solar thought) took place in Egypt, followed later by the advent of a lesser peak in Monomotapa.

6.4 Delivery of fetishes to M'vûmbi Mbumbulu

The M'vûmbi Mbumbulu, the straying of the Bantu and the hibernation of their civilizations began with the scattering of tribes from Zimbabwe, followed by the eclipse which began with the arrival of the Arabs and

---

[43] *Le sorcier de la pluie chez les Batonga* (Echo d'Afrique, octobre 1910, p. 150).
[44] Van Wing, J., *Etudes Bakongo*, Léopoldville, 1938. p. 419.

Westerners on continent; because this eruption of lunar civilizations forced the Blacks to abandon solar values.

There was therefore a need to prepare the offspring for its survival during this period of tempered initiatory activity resulting in the absence of the Nzala Mpânda. Thus, since the great initiatory knowledge and power that had been the glory of ancestors at the Nzala Mpânda would be dormant, it should be left to mankind a simple but palliative approach: the fetish resulting from the transfer of divine power through mere faith. To do this, Nzala Mpânda gave to M'vûmbi Mbumbulu very powerful fetishes. But we must recognize that although powerful, these fetishes can never equal the divine *n'kisi* of Nzala Mpânda, they therefore can not fulfill all his prowesses.

6.5   The Africa of the eclipse

And soon it is the eclipse that falls on the Black African nation; the Blacks are straying in the domination of the lunar thought and do not know how to find their way: they are in confusion, chaos and even stagnation, if not regression. The Black man forced to ape the Western and the Arab is neither a White in black skin nor a real Black; he lost all Black African identity and no longer knows where to stand. And this unfortunate situation only relegates him to the last position, the background of the scientific and technological activity: his name is thus M'vûmbi Mbumbulu, which characterizes the state of one who is lost in a night of reduced activity.

However, as any rule matches exceptions, it is found in the M'vûmbi Mbumbulu people who still remember the solar path, the path followed by their ancestors. The myth tells us that fixing their gaze firmly to the heavens, to the abode of illuminated ancestors, i.e., clinging to solar approach, these visionaries "looking at the sky, there they discern a path and then suddenly one of them rises and disappears with arms extended. Nzala Mpânda had come to take him." These visionaries have finally found the way of their ancestors, the path to the high Black African spirituality, a spirituality that is the key of the Nzala Mpânda.

These visionaries, solitary stars in the darkened sky, indicating the pole of the high Afrocentric spirituality, have a duty to prepare their Black Africans brothers so they can get out of the bondage of the lunar civilization, and find the path leading to the future Nzala Mpânda; because the myth says, although he died a second time, Nzala Mpânda had finally risen and had ascended to the ancestors from which he will return again someday to help Black African humanity, which currently is totally benighted.

6.6   Nzala Mpânda in the third millennium

It is this future advent of Nzala Mpânda which was prophesied by the big Black Messiah, the prophet Simon Kimbangu in these terms: "The Black man will become White and the White man will become Black; for the spiritual and moral foundations, as we know them today, will be profoundly shaken. Wars will persist worldwide. The Kongo will be free and Africa too."[45] The

---

[45] Kiatezua Lubanzadio Luyaluka, *la Religion kôngo*, Paris: l'Harmattan, 2010, p. 147.

great Kongo prophet teaches us that the next coming of the Nzala Mpânda is an imminent event which awaits our generation, according to the Kongo foreknowledge.

7   LESSONS LEARNED FROM MYTH

The myth of Nzala Mpânda allows us to draw several lessons; they concern the origin of fetishes, their temporary nature, and their destiny which implies their abandonment in favor of the awakening of the high Black African spirituality; spirituality is the key of the Nzala Mpânda. The myth also shows us the fleeting and limited nature of the lunar thought in which the black man is now mired.

7.1   Fetishes come from the divine mystery

After exposing the myth, van Wing draws his own conclusion by stating that: "In a sense we could say that this myth is only a fictionalized expression of the thought that have been expressed to me by many elders interviewed on the origin of *min'kisi*: "it is Nzâmbi who gave *n'kisi* [human, fetishes,] to our elders."[46]

Thus, as I said above and in accordance with the deep tradition, the myth of Nzala Mpânda tells us that fetishes are rooted in the divine mystery. However in the spirit of the ancients, the use of fetishes must be circumscribed in time.

---

[46] Van Wing, J., *Etudes Bakongo*, Léopoldville, 1938. pp. 419-420.

7.2   The fetishes are temporary

The fetishes are a temporary and palliative means that the need of spiritual growth impels us to abandon today; this is one of the conditions for the Black Africans' revival of the Nzala Mpânda. They must put their trust completely in the Most High God that their illuminated ancestors served and not in human and demonic *min'kisi* and this need is even more urgent for their elite.

It is obvious that the divine mystery and the demonic cannot coalesce. Thus a materialistic civilization, like the western, is based on the couple human-demonic, while the spiritual based Kôngo civilization was anchored on the couple divine-human.

Therefore, the action of spirituality is not the destruction of the human elements, but their elevation. True African divine mystery works for the elevation of the use of the human *n'kisi* and the destruction of the demonic ones, because this last can only be of evil use. However this action cannot be efficient unless the spiritual elite abandons even the palliative use of the human fetish to firmly anchor its faith on the divine.

Van Wing shows us that the necessity of abandoning fetishes was well understood by the Bakongo. The first evidence that can be drawn from the study of van Wing on understanding of the need for this abandonment is that the great figures of the Kongo spiritual tradition of the time of the M'vûmbi Mbumbulu, namely Apolonia Mafuta, Kimpa Vita[47] and Simon Kimbangu, advocated abandoning all *min'kisi* and the masses obeyed them without hesitation.

About abandoning the *min'kisi* van Wing remark: "When Kimbangu, acknowledged savior of his people, imposed the destruction of *min'kisi* he was obeyed not only by his aware members but by the entire populations, which did not had direct contact with him and his followers. And before that, during the movement Kiyoka triggered in northern Angola to 1872, all the fetishes were burned (yoka) with enthusiasm."[48]

The Kongo people therefore understood that the fetishes were to be abandoned one day. But the Bakongo knew that conversely, the divine mystery and its cults to Nzâmbi Ampûngu Tulêndo through the intercession of saint-ancestors never had to be abandoned. And even in cases where they have unfortunately agreed to abandon them van Wing highlights the reluctance of the Blacks in these terms: "It was a capital case, requiring negotiations and endless explanations to bury the bin of the ancestors!" This reluctance of the Besikôngo is justified insofar as the bin of the ancestors symbolized the centuries-old religion bequeathed to them by the Ancients, which is not the case for the fetishes.

It is possible that this understanding of the necessity and the imminent abandonment of any *min'kisi* by the spiritual elite and of demonic *min'kisi* by everyone was

---

[47] Margaret Washington, *Le Legs universel de Kimpa Vita aux peuples noirs*, http /pbs.org/wgbh/aia/part1/1i3077.
[48] Van Wing, J., *Etudes Bakongo*, Léopoldville, 1938. p. 422.

the element that has led some Kongo kings to easily abandon their fetish to embrace the Christian faith.

7.3 The lunar thought is a limitation

Another great lesson that the myth of Nzala Mpânda teaches us philosophically is that the lunar thought, in which the Black African man is now mired, is a great epistemological limitation of knowledge and power. The lunar thought can never match the prowess awaiting us ahead if we return to the solar thought. But we can not go back to the solar thinking as long as we are mired in an epistemological approach (western approach) which is not adapted to our profound thinking.

This myth also implies that the reign of fetishes are palliative, they are expected to disappear to leave the way to the high solar science. The Black African scientist and philosopher must prepare for the advent of the solar thinking, and work to understand the epistemological bases of this thought which are different from those of the lunar thought that fascinates us today due to the lack of sufficient knowledge of our own epistemological culture.

The new advent of solar thought requires of the Black man the abandonment of the fetish in favor of the exercise of the Black African high spirituality. That's why great figures of the Black African initiation of our time (Apolonia Mafuta, Kimpa Vita, Simon Kimbangu, etc..) All worked to persuade their kinsmen to abandon fetishes in favor of the true religion of their ancestors.

8   THE NZALA MPÂNDA IN EGYPT

The interpretation of the myth of Nzala Mpânda, as I have just described it, can be well integrated with other elements of the history of Ancient Egypt and the migration of Bantu peoples; especially when one considers that migration according to the hypothesis sustained by Batshikama et al, hypothesis that it took place from the west to the south of the continent finally back from the west to the center of the Africa.

Batshikama affirms the Egyptian origins of the Bantu in these terms: "Among the Semitic peoples, continues D. P. de Pedrals, were also the Hebrews (Khabir) or Israelite. Certain in conditions universally known, settled in Egypt; others are later found in Ethiopia. But while the latter in favor of the dynastic union of Makeda and Solomon, spreading beliefs and Jewish institutions and make Ethiopia an active partner companies of the kings of Jerusalem and Tyre, the other had, probably due to the failure of the designs of the same order, choose to withdraw from Egypt and to return to the country of origin. The author concludes: this eastern invasion that caused the ascension of some Black tribes of Nubia and to the very gates of the kingdom of Thebes, was probably, in fact, the cause also of great upheaval that would lead to the meeting of Pygmies, Bushmen and Hottentots primitive black populations whose current block called Bantu likely originated."[49]

---

[49] Batshikama ba Mampuya ma Ndwala, R., *Voici les Jagas*, Kinshasa, 1971, p. 267.

It is by starting from this assumption of an Egyptian origin of the Bantu that I'll explain the two advents of the Nzala Mpânda the pinnacle of Black Africans initiatory knowledge and power.

8.1 Mysteries of Egypt

One of the first implications of this interpretation of the myth of Nzala Mpânda in connection with the history of ancient Egypt is that there was in this nation a education system of initiatory kind in which existed the divine mystery; for the divine mystery is the key to the Nzala Mpânda, as I pointed out above.

The hypothesis of the existence of two mysteries in ancient Egypt exists without a shadow of doubt among Egyptologists. They all allude to the existence of the great and little mysteries in the land of the Pharaohs. Speaking of the existence of these two mysteries Massey emphasizes that: "The greater mysteries are eschatological and religious."[50] The great mystery was a mystery which prepared the prophets, this is reflected in the importance of oracles in the Egyptian system.

Thus, unlike the great mystery, the little mysteries tackled all aspects of science to facilitate the lives of the population and its protection. Although still focused on the divine, the little mysteries regrouped in fact all human knowledge.

This division allows me to say with certainty that there were ultimately three mysteries in Egypt: the

---

[50] Massey, *Ancient Egypt the light of the world*, www.masseiana.org.

divine mystery, the martial mystery and the civil mystery. This statement does not, however, contradicts the Egyptologists when they emphasize the existence of the great and little mysteries in Egypt; because Egyptology recognizes that the military formed a separate caste. Maspero in his book on Egypt states: "The power of Pharaoh and his barons rested entirely upon these two classes, the priests and the soldiers."[51] One can also read this in the book *Ancient Egypt* by. Rawlinson: "Each summer he visited the place, to see their supplies of corn measured out for his soldiers and their pay delivered to them, as well as to superintend their military exercises, in order that foreigners might hold them in respect."[52]

Talking about the benefits of the soldiers in Egypt, Herodotus abounds in the same direction and says of them: "The following privilege was specially granted to this class and to none others of the Egyptians except the priests, that is to say, each man had twelve yokes of land specially granted to him free from imposts." [53]

This concern of the Pharaoh for his soldiers and the fact that they were a very important class next to the priests, coupled to the initiatory nature of the training offered by the Egyptians education system, allows me to assert that like the priests, the soldiers formed in the small mystery, a separate initiatory caste.

---

[51] Maspero, *History of Egypt Chaldea, Syria, Babylonia, and Assyria*, vol. 2. www.gutenberg.org.

[52] Rawlinson, G., *Ancient Egyt*, www.gutenberg.org.

[53] Hérodote, *An account of Egypt*, www.gutenberg.org.

So can I conclude that in the little mystery there was the martial mystery and the civil mystery, as we have seen in the initiatory system of the Kongo kingdom. The great mystery, the martial mystery and the civil mystery thus formed three sides of the tetrahedral pyramid of Egyptian initiatory knowledge and power.

8.2   Nzala Mpânda in Egypt

The presence of these three mysteries was essential to the progress of Egypt, and we will see later that cut off the quintessence of priestly mystery Egypt could only sink into weakness.

In my hypothesis, therefore, the first Nzala Mpânda took place in Egypt, as I noted above. Mackenzie confirms my assertion because he writes: "When "Cleopatra's Needle" was erected by Thothmes III, the Conqueror, and the forerunner of Alexander the Great and Napoleon, Egyptian civilization had attained its highest level."[54] This is the first of the two peaks alluded in the myth of Nzala Mpânda. I have demonstrated that the events referred to by the myth took place before the establishment of the kingdom of Kongo and in a place where the Bantu ethnics met. It is thus easy to say that these places can only be Zimbabwe or Egypt which are the two major population centers of the Bantu before their last dispersal preceding that of slavery.

---

[54] Donald Mackenzie, *Egyptian Myth and Legend*, www.sacred-texts.com.

9   THE COUNTRY OF PUNT

One of the enigmas which Egyptologists face is the land of Punt[55] which is alluded in history. Before the reign of Pharaoh Thutmose III, reign during which Egypt reached its peak, the regency was in the hands of Queen Hatshepsut[56]. One of the events that marked this regency is an expedition sent to the land of Punt, but the location of this mythical country is a matter of disagreement among scholars of the history of ancient Egypt.

Speaking of this travel Rawlinson says that the fleet weighed anchor and "sailed down the Red Sea, borne by favourable winds, which were ascribed to the gracious majesty of Ammon, and reached their destination, the Ta-neter, or "Holy Land"—the "abode of Athor," and perhaps the original home of Ammon himself—without accident or serious difficulty."[57]

It should be noted that the country of Punt is called, in the account of the expedition of Hatshepsut, the "Holy Land"[58], it is the abode of God Hathor, and is believed to be the birthplace of the god Ammon. Maspero notes that: "Further, the word Punt is always written without the hieroglyph determinative of a foreign country, thus showing that the Egyptians did not regard the Punites

---

[55] Some authors say Puanit or Puanta.

[56] Certains auteurs écrivent plutôt Hatasu.

[57] Rawlinson, G., *Ancient Egyt,* www.gutenberg.org.

[58] Diop in *Antériorité des civilisations nègres* (p. 55) translates this term by To-noutir and explains this expression as signifying « the land of the Gods", however even in this denotation an allusion is made to a holy land.

as foreigners."[59] This shows that the Punt, to the eyes of the Egyptians, was thus inhabited by people who were close with them to the point of not being considered foreign; so it was the root population from which their ancestors left.

Here I digress by pointing out that the Bible says in his stories the sixth verse of the tenth chapter of Genesis: "The son of Ham: Cush, Mizraim, Put and Canaan." We know that Cush is the current Sudan Mistraïm is the biblical name for Egypt and Puth (or punt) is presented as his brother; here this more clearly explains the fact that the Egyptians did not consider the people of Punt as foreigners: they were their brothers like the Nubians.

Speaking of the inhabitants of Punt Maspero describes them as looking like the Egyptians as follows: "the native belonged to a light-coloured race, and the portraits we possess of them resemble the Egyptian type in every particular. They are tall and thin, and of colour which varied between-brick red and the darkest brown."[60]

However, to better understand the importance of Rawlinson's assertion that the Punt is the "abode of Athor," the "the original home of Ammon", we must first understand the concept of divinity in the religion of Egypt.

---

[59] Maspero, *History of Egypt Chaldea, Syria, Babylonia, and Assyria Vol. 4*, www.gutenberg.org.
[60] Maspero, *History* of Egypt Chaldea, Syria, Babylonia, and Assyria, Vol. 4 www.gutenberg.org.

Contrary to what many Egyptologists say, the Egyptian conception of God implied a belief in a hierarchy of deities above which was a Supreme Being, the principle of existence, that the Egyptians did not dare name. In reference maybe to a first principle of existence in the Egyptian cosmogony, Cheik Anta Diop talks about Kepher the principle of becoming that precedes the Creator God Ra.[61]

In his book *Ancient Egypt*, Rawlinson wrote: "Besides the common popular religion, the belief of the masses, there was another which prevailed among the priests and among the educated. The primary doctrine of this esoteric religion was the real essential unity of the Divine Nature. The sacred texts, known only to the priests and to the initiated, taught that there was a single Being, "the sole producer of all things both in heaven and earth, himself not produced of any," "the only true living God, self-originated," "who exists from the beginning," "who has made all things, but has not himself been made." This Being seems never to have been represented by any material, even symbolical, form."[62]

So those who attribute the polytheistic nature to the Egyptian religion dot it may be because they judge this religion from the opinion of the masses, rather than from the opinions of elected and the elite as does Rawlinson; for this bad approach is often the one anthropology

---

[61] Cheik Anta Diop, *Antériorité des civilisations nègres*, Présence africaine, Abidjan, 1972, p 217.
[62] Rawlinson, G., *Ancient Egyt,* www.gutenberg.org.

used in the study of "primitive's" civilizations, and even any religion other than Christianity.

If I'm totally of the opinion of Rawlinson, I have, however, for scientific honesty to point out a contrary hypothesis, in fact, Archibald Henry Sayce says in his book *Religion of the ancient Egypt and Babylonia*: "There are indeed literary monuments rescued from the wreck of ancient Egyptian culture which embody the highest and most spiritual conceptions of the Godhead, and use the language of the purest monotheism. But such monuments represent the beliefs and ideas of the cultured few rather than of the Egyptians as a whole, or even of the majority of the educated classes." [63]

The paradigm of those who see in Egypt only polytheism is that the monotheism which is visible there is only the opinion of a certain elite, if not a failed attempt of Akhenaton, while to get an idea of the Egyptian religion one must stick to the opinion of the majority. Here the obvious question is: if a researcher wants to understand the deep thought of a modern religion which thought will he inquire that of the elite or the mass? It goes without saying that it is the thought of the minority who specializes in this religion which will be the interest of the researcher. So why when it comes to study a pre-Christian religion do people use the opposite paradigm? Egypt has always been a monotheistic nation; this is why all religions that came

---

[63] Sayce, A. H., *the Religion of ancient Egypt and Babylonia*, www.gutenberg.org.

from this nation, Judaism and Black-African religions, are all monotheistic.

Some may ask me the following questions: what is then called Akhenaton's reform? Was it not an attempt to move from polytheism to monotheism? My answer to this last question is naturally negative. The uniqueness of the Supreme Being, does not imply the uniqueness of the nomenclature of the Gods, as indeed can be seen by considering the Black African ethnics, who accept that they worship the same God Most High. This implies that, although in the hierarchy each nome of Egypt had its God, his guardian spirit, the same sun God, the creator, was designated under different names.

Akhenaton, ranking himself above the considerations of the individualities of nomes, has opted that his citizens must invoke the Most High God through the sun God (to be called by Aton by all) and not everyone through the God of his nome. Thus, such a decision did not constitute an attempt to establish monotheism, but rather an attempt to unify nomes under one protective spirit and to unify the appellation of the solar God. This is also what explains the fact that this position of the pharaoh Akhenaton did not survive his reign: fundamentally his reform brought nothing new to the Egyptian religion.

In the real Egyptian religion, above the Creator God represented by the solar disk there was therefore a Supreme Being, the principle of life, who was neither named nor represented by the scribes. Thus, those so-called Gods in Egypt are they only manifestations of this

Supreme Being; they are only holy-ancestors, to use a properly African speaking.

Starting from this conception of deity, Thoth, the great initiator of the Osirian religion, taught to Egyptians initiates: "Men are mortal Gods and Gods are immortal men."[64] The land of Punt was seen as the home of the ancestors of the Egyptians, and the land where their ancestors left to reach the borders of the Mediterranean. And Punt was for the Egyptians the Holy Land, or the land "flowing with milk and honey". Thus, Punt is the place where the Egyptians had to go back after leaving the Nile.

As I noted above, Egyptologists are not unanimous on the location of the country of Punt. Some of them put this mythical country in Arabia, however, this assumption is contradicted by the fact that some of the products brought by the expedition sent by Hatshepsut could not come from Arabia. Rawlinson emphasizes this fact by stating that: ""Punt" has been generally identified with Southern Arabia, and it is certainly in favour of this view that the chief object of the expedition was to procure incense and spices, which Arabia is known to have produced anciently in profusion. But among the other products of the land mentioned in the inscriptions of Hatasu, there are several which Arabia could not possibly have furnished."[65] These products that Arabia could not provide probably included: the tips of ivory, leopard skins, ebony...

---

[64] Schuré, E., *les Grands initiés*, Perrin, Paris, 1970, p. 159.
[65] Rawlinson, G., *Ancient Egyt,* www.gutenberg.org.

One thing is certain: the country of Punt was located south of Egypt and could be reached after several days of sailing through the Red Sea. Thus some Egyptologists believe that the Land of Punt should be near Somalia. However, Cheik Anta Diop puts the Punt to Zimbabwe[66].

Besides the hypothesis of Diop is also found that Massey who writes: "But the land of Puanta is also geographical, and there was an Egyptian tradition that this divine country could be reached by ascending the river Nile. It was reported that in a remote region south you came to an unknown great water which bathed Puanta or the holy land, Ta-nuter. This, we suggest, was that nearest and largest of all the African lakes, now called the Victoria[67]."[68]

Moreover, in another book, Massey says: "It is possible that the first intellectual beginnings of the first race and of the Egyptians themselves were about the sources of the Nile."[69] Diop also believes that the Egyptians saw the South as the land of their origins; He supports this argument by writing of the Egyptians: "They still remembered that their ancestors came from the south, as the Ethiopians also claimed of their origin. In the ritual, the South had always priority over the North. The Egyptian oriented his move by turning to the

---

[66] Cheik Anta Diop, *Antériorité des civilisations nègres*, Présence africaine, Abidjan, 1972, p 25 b.

[67] The lake Victoria is now called Tanganyika.

[68] Massey, *Ancient Egypt light of the world*, www.masseiana.org.

[69] Massey, *Book of the begining*, www.masseiana.org.

south, the country from where came his gods and his ancestors. "[70]

The assumptions of Diop and Massey allow me to conclude that the country of Punt could not be other than the basin of Central Africa, a region worthy of being described as the land "flowing with milk and honey", a country of immense resources. It is therefore from the heart of Africa that the Egyptians left to live on the shores of the Mediterranean, knowing that they would return one day to their homeland. Referring to a cultural similarity between Central Africa and the Punt Maspero wrote of the wife of the Chief of the country of Punt: "She was endowed with a type of beauty much admired by the people of Central Africa, being so inordinately fat that the shape of her body was scarcely recognizable under the rolls of flesh which hung down from t"[71]

So I think the expedition of Hatshepsut to Zimbabwe prepared an exodus of Egyptians to the south, to the heart of Africa. This exodus therefore marks the end of the first Nzala Mpânda. And, as I said above, Mackenzie abounds in the same direction as he writes: "When "Cleopatra's Needle" was erected by Thothmes III, the Conqueror, and the forerunner of Alexander the Great and Napoleon, Egyptian civilization had attained

---

[70] Cheik Anta Diop, *Antériorité des civilisations nègres*, Présence africaine, Abidjan, 1972, p. 54.
[71] Maspero, *History of Egypt Chaldea, Syria, Babylonia, and Assyria,* Vol. 4 www.gutenberg.org.

its highest level."[72] Now Thutmose reigned just after Hatshepsut.

Further archaeological excavations have revealed the presence in the region of Zimbabwe of elements belonging to the Egyptian civilization. Diop wrote about this: "A statuette of Osiris was found in Congo "Leo"[73] at Mulongo dating from approximately -800. Another statuette of Osiris with a cartridge of Thutmose III (-1450) was also found south of the Zambezi. "[74]

The Egyptians, aware that the sleep of their initiatory power that would ensue was temporary, that it will be followed by the advent of a second Nzala Mpânda, and being aware of the great hibernation awaiting them in horizon, they decided to hide what they had of most precious: the divine mystery. They consciously prepared themselves for the end of the supremacy of their knowledge and power as a man secures his property before going to sleep.

It is normal to attribute such wisdom and such foreknowledge to the Egyptians as long as Thoth, the great initiator of all their wisdom, taught them: "In the time that comes, will be seen a reversal of values and an alteration of wisdom for those who will take your place on this star. (...)

---

[72] Donald Mackenzie, *Egyptian Myth and Legend*, www.sacred-texts.com.
[73] L'actuel République démocratique du Congo.
[74] Cheik Anta Diop, *Antériorité des civilisations nègres*, Présence africaine, Abidjan, 1972, p. 55.

"Many who are chained in darkness will try to prevent others from rising into light. This will cause a great war that will shake the earth and shake it in its course.

"The Brothers of darkness will cause a conflict between light and darkness."[75]

The wisdom of the Egyptians was therefore dictated by the need to prepare for this conflict between light and darkness, between the solar thought and the lunar thought, conflict symbolized in the myth of Nzala Mpânda by the eclipse[76]. It is this final conflict that the prophet Simon Kimbangu speaks when he invokes Nzâmbi Ampûngu Tulêndo in these words: "Come! Oh! God, the Father Almighty! I call you, and all the angels of war (*mbasi za mvita*) to lead a fight against this dark world (*nsi a bûbu*)!

"Woe to those who continue to strengthen slavery and colonization of Black people! You are a living God. I implore you constantly (*Ngieti ku fiongonena*) on behalf of the shed blood of all your Sent and their humiliation. I ask you and I recommend you, O! God of Love (Kalunga): Come with Your angels of the heavens and the earth to destroy the humanity of Darkness (*mahânza my kibûbu*) which continues to mock your majestic Love! "[77]

---

[75] *Le Chemin d'Hermès*, www.lescheminsdhermes.org.

[76] Dans l'imaginaire populaire, l'éclipse est perçue comme une lutte entre la lune et le soleil.

[77] Kiatezua L.L. *la Religion kôngo*, Paris : l'Harmattan, 2010, p. 150.

Black people of Africa and of the Diaspora, are you ready for the fight for your final liberation from the benightedness? It is to this task that the Kongo prophets of old and of today call you, because for the enlightened minds, the brief reign of the lunar thought is already nearing its end.

10 THE EXODUS OF THE BANTU

One of the hypotheses that I advance here is that the great mystery in Egypt was mainly the task of the Bantu; the martial mystery was the focus of warrior ethnics that inhabit today Western Africa, while the Nilotic ethnics excelled mainly in the civil mystery.

According to my hypothesis, the first waves of Egyptians who headed to the Promised Land were the Bantu; in other words the Bantu took care of the priestly mystery in Egypt. This assertion is based on the following facts:

- The warrior ethnics of the West and the Nilotic are the last to reach the Taneter, the heart of Africa; they were all preceded by the Bantu. Now the heart of Africa was for the Egyptians the Promised Land, it is thus toward this land that the three initiatory castes of the country of the Pharaohs converged.

- That the warrior ethnics of West Africa are the last to have left Egypt is affirmed by the fact that some of their languages have kept their affinity with that of Egypt. This is the case for Wolof as demonstrated by Cheik Anta Diop.[78]

------

[78] Cf., Cheik Anta Diop, *Antériorité des civilisations nègres*, Présence africaine, Abidjan, 1972,

- There is a striking similarity between the drawings of Egyptian priests and the attitudes of the Bakôngo. Massey spoke of it in these terms: " Of the Congos, Bastian says, 'When they spoke to a superior they might have sat as models to the Egyptian priests when making the representations on the temple walls, so striking is the likeness between what is there depicted and what actually takes place here.' Theirs were the primitive sketches, the Egyptians finished the pictures."[79]

- We have seen that according to Rawlinson, the Egyptians never represented the Supreme Being-. Now van Wing points to the same attitude among the Bakôngo: they never represented Nzâmbi Ampûngu Tulêndo.[80]

- The legacy of the great mystery allowed the Bantu, mainly the Bakôngo, to be the fertile ground from which sprang the great figures of the high Black African spirituality, powerful prophets by their spiritual height and their works, prophets worthy of the great initiatory tradition as represented in the Bible: Nsasukulu N'kanda, Kodi Puanga, Tuti dia Tiya, Apollonia Mafuta, Kimpa Vita, Mbumba Philippe, Simon Kimbangu…

- As holders of the great mystery, the Bantu, especially the Bakôngo, were able to restore the three mysteries of the Egyptian initiation; and thus do we find among these Black Africans: the great mystery represented by the Kimpasi as a school of divine prophets, the martial mystery which was alive in the Kinkimba and the civil mystery taught in the Lemba.

- Opposite to the Bakôngo, the ethnics of Western Africa as the holders of martial mystery could not restore the three mysteries in their system; On the contrary, due the preponderance of the martial mystery, the serpent, which is the symbol of martial strength as I have shown above, is finally deified; this explains the current form of the Voodoo.

---

[79] Massey, *Book of the beginning*, www.masseiana.org.
[80] Van Wing, J., *Etudes Bakôngo*, Léopoldville, 1938, p. 305.

Once the Bantu came out of Egypt, the country temporarily remained in the hands of the little mystery which included the martial and the civil mysteries.

11 EGYPT OF THE BIBLE

Here a question may arise, if as I assert the strength of the ancient Egypt was in its mastery of the divine mystery, why does the Bible shows it as being rather mired in the human, if not demonic mystery, in front of the prowesses of Moses?

The story of the exodus of the Hebrew from Egypt calls for some caution in its examination. In his book titled *Moïse, l'Africain* Nillon[81] Pierre explains that there is a distinction to be made between the Israelites and the Jews. The biblical story of the exodus is a syncretism in which are entangled two stories: the expulsion of the Hebrew by the pharaoh Ahmoses and not Ramses as the biblical anachronism has it, and the flight of the Israelites under the leadership of Moses.

11.1 The exodus expulsion

One can read in the Bible: "the Egyptians were urgent upon the people, that they might send them out of the land in haste." Exodus 12: 33. This is the account of the expulsion of the Hebrew (called Hyksos in the record of the ancient Egyptians) who seized the power of Pharaoh and with the cunning of Joseph enslaved the Egyptians on their own land. The Hebrews were finally

---

[81] Pierre, N., *Moïse, l'Africain*, Paris. Menaibuc 2001

expelled from Egypt by the might of the pharaoh Ahmoses.

11.2 The exodus flight

The second exodus is, according to Nillon Pierre, that of the Israelites. The Bible says: "And it was told the king of Egypt that the people fled." (Exodus 14:5). This exodus is the outcome of the failure of the attempted reform of Akhenaton. Due to his hatred of the priests of Ammon, the pharaoh was despised by his people. He retreated in his new capital city of Akhetaton with his followers.

Despite the succor of the Hebrews (under the promise of the restoration to this later of the city of Avaris), the followers of Akhenaton and their allies were obliged to flee in the desert under the leadership of a priest of Osiris named Osarsiph who came to be known as Moses.

The Jews stems from the Hebrews, they are Semites, while the Israelites are Egyptians. The Hebrews adopted the language and the divinities of the Canaanites. This later detail is illustrated by the fact that Abraham paid a dime to Melchisedek a Canaanite king and high priest; an act which clearly shows that the Abraham adopted the religion of the Egyptian king (the Canaanites being brothers of Egyptian), or he was supportive of his religion. The modern Israeli archeology demonstrates that up to the third century before the Christian era the Jews were still worshipping Egyptian Gods.

Thus the true rendition of the story of the Bible does not lead to the conclusion of the weakness of the Egyptian divine mystery, but rather to its final adoption by the Hebrews.

12 THE NZALA MPÂNDA ZIMBABWE

Western historians were long puzzled by the buildings they found on the site of the ruins of the ancient kingdom of Monomotapa. According to their archaeological expertise, these monuments could only be the work of the Egyptians or people who drew their inspiration from the high science of Egyptian initiatory academies. However, their intelligence, refused to attribute these structures to the Bantu, because it would prove their Egyptian origin; now in their eyes, the Bantu were only primitive peoples. These Western historians have never been able to find where their Egyptian builders had gone, because in reality they were not other than the Bantu who came from the north of the Black continent.

Speaking of these constructions, called by indigenous Zimbabwes, the author of the General History of Africa writes: "It is true that the granite of this region can be cut in regular blocks; these builders were not so exceptional technicians belonging to a superior civilization, as have dreamed esoteric historians. It seems that these people, Chonas (possibly Bantu) were also from the north. "[82]

----

[82] Dumont, J., *L'histoire générale de l'Afrique*, Paris, 1972, p.91.

So after leaving Egypt, the Bantu still kept in some extent the expertise they had developed on the shores of the Nile, and it is this expertise that they have used for the building of these amazing stone monuments.

The second Nzala Mpânda occurred in Zimbabwe. These citadels of stone that surprised Western explorers are one of the indelible marks that the myth of Nzala Mpânda speaks about; fingerprints destined to remind the Black Africans their glorious past.

12.1 The dispersion of the Bantu

The step of Zimbabwe does not however constitute the final destination of the Egyptians. Because soon, the Nzala Mpânda being gone for the second time, the Bantu ethnics would start the last trip toward their final destinations. In this final march to their current land, the key of the Nzala Mpânda would eventually be brought by the Bakôngo in the place marked by the destiny, while awaiting its pending future use, i.e., imminent, for the awakening of Black African nation.

This is may be what led Franz Fanon to argue that "Africa has the shape of a gun whose trigger is in Congo."[83] But whoever pays a keen attention on the map of Africa will realize that the trigger of the famous gun is precisely at Kongo-Central[84]. Thus it is from this geographical point of the continent that spiritual light will

---

[83] Cité par le Président Mobutu Sese Seko dans son discours à l'ONU en 1973.
[84] La province congolaise du Bas-Congo.

dawn to extend throughout Africa and toward the Diaspora.

12.2 The passage Nzôndo and loss of the *sengele mbêle*

The dispersion of Black African ethnics from Zimbabwe can be compared to another myth spread in the milieu of the Lemba and indicating that it took place after the passage of Nzôndo and the loss of *sengele mbêle*.[85] Nzôndo is a mythical character who has only one eye, one ear, one arm and one leg, the Black African Cyclops. However, despite his apparent handicap, Nzôndo is very powerful and is able to go around the world in the blink of an eye!

Fukiau wrote in his book *le Mukôngo et le monde qui l'entourait*, about the myth of Nzôndo: "Our ancestors first settled in Zimba and remained there until after the passage of Nzondo they lost the "*mbele nsengele*" (saber without handle), a sign of knowledge, work, power, authority and dignity. As soon as the news of the loss of the *nsengele* was known they dispersed, or "*banwa maza ma nzenza.*""[86] This last expression literally means "they drank foreign waters."

The Nzôndo alluded in this myth is a mysterious power whose passage leads to a disruption of the dynamic order of the universe. Fukiau explains: "The passage of this fabulous character had as effect the

---

[85] A saber symbolizing authority.

[86] Fukiau, A., *le Mukongo et le monde qui l'entourait*, Kinshasa, 1969, p. 116.

material, moral and intellectual regression of the people."[87]

The myth emphasizes that the passage of Nzôndo happened at Zimba, a locality that Fukiau assimilates to Zimbabwe. It is thus due to this passage of the mysterious being that the Bantu have lost the *sengele mbêle* symbol of scientific and technological authority, and this loss was the triggering sign of their dispersion.

However we know that the highest authority in the solar thought is the one conferred by the divine mystery; thus the loss of *sengele mbêle* at Zimbabwe is none other than the loss of the higher mastery of the great spirituality essential factor of the power of solar thought. This also implies that the Nzala Mpânda was a factor of the unity of the Black African masses, whereas the loss of the authority it confers could only lead to disorders, desolation and even dispersion.

12.3 The hypothesis Batshikama

About this myth of Nzôndo, Batshikama gives another interpretation in his book *Voici les Jaga.*[88]. According to him, the appearance of Nzôndo is a historical fact. Nzôndo had buildt the city of Zimba north-east of the city of Luozi [a Kongo city of the Democratic Republic of Congo]. This city had been ruined due to the troubles that took place there following the loss of the Sengele Mbêle. This Sengele "was a" girl without a husband," i.e., a virgin, who entered the

---

[87] Fukiau, ibidem, p. 116.

[88] Batshikama, R., *Voici les Jagas, Kinshasa*, 1971, pp. 213-214.

initiatory room (*wakota bukûmbi*), and had mysteriously disappeared the day when his training was complete, when she was due to be released."

As for me, I would lean toward the hypothesis of Fukiau: the Nzôndo is a mythical character who symbolizes a dynamic change in the universe. In favor of this hypothesis of Fukiau, I can provide the fact that we find the same mythical figure in the culture of Kasai Occidental under the name N'kuembe. The Baluba of this region of the Democratic Republic of Congo consider N'kuembe as a force capable of bringing great dynamic changes in the universe.

It is therefore logical to argue that the two Bantu traditions on this mythical character must be related to a common locus of dispersion which in this case can only be located upstream of the creation of the Kingdom of Kongo. This should be the case especially when we know that, considering the migration of the Bantu ethnics from Zimbabwe, the migration of the Luba peoples from Zimbabwe was made directly to their current locations while the Bakôngo were forced to go down to the Southern Africa before turning northward by the west coast. And the common locus of dispersion which must be attached to the myth of Nzôndo can not be other than the Zimba, thus the Zimbabwe.

12.4 The delivery of fetishes to Mvumbi Mbumbulu

I demonstrated above that, as myths similar to that of Nzala Mpânda are found among other ethnics, this myth, as far as the Bantu are concerned, refers to events that took place before the creation of the Kingdom of Kongo; i.e., before the Kongo dia Tuku which is the original country of the Bakôngo. This similarity of myths implies the existence of a point of departure, which is the center of diffusion. Thus it is from Zimbabwe, the last outbreak of the Bantu dispersion before the arrival of Westerners, that we must place the delivery of "powerful *n'kisi*" to Mvûmbi Mbumbulu.

It is more plausible to locate the giving of the powerful fetishes to Mvumbi Mbumbulu at Zimbabwe because the Batonga, that other people who mention the myth similar to the myth of Nzala Mpânda in their tradition, remained on the earth of the dispersion. Always aware of the prophecies left to them by their ancestors engaged in the divine mystery, the Bantu knew that with the loss of the *sengele mbêle* would ensue the decrease of the initiatory power whereby it would be necessary for the population to have a palliative means for their protection, while awaiting the return of the pending Nzala Mpânda from heaven, i.e., through divine revelation, and these palliative means are fetishes.

13 THE M'VUMBI MBUMBULU IN THE KINGDOM OF KONGO

I showed above that among the Bantu, the Bakôngo were able to reproduce, but also keep intact the three mysteries (the Kimpasi - the priestly mystery in the South, the Kinkimba – martial mystery to the West, and the Lemba – the civil mystery at the north). That's why they have the daunting task of helping other Africans in restoring the tetrahedral pyramid of Black African spirituality; they are the trigger of the gun of Fanon that is Africa.

The Bakôngo thus constitute the quintessence of the Egyptians priestly caste. This explains the fury of the forces of darkness against their kingdom. However, one thing is undeniably true: the arrival on the costs of the Kongo of the Portuguese navigator Diego Cao in the fifteenth century marked the beginning of the eclipse of M'vûmbi Mbumbulu among the Bantu. Because, from that moment, the entire spiritual culture of Black African man would receive, of invaders from overseas, the stigma of demonization.

In accepting the scholastic Christian faith at the arrival of Westerners in the 15th century, but especially by denying the religion of his ancestors that he believed to be fundamentally different from the true teachings of the Bible, King Nzinga Nkuwu sounded the death knell of the end of the brightness of the solar thought; brightness which was then seen in the prosperity of his kingdom. The kingdom of Kongo would soon sink into chaos, despite the burst of pride of King M'vemb'a N'zinga (called also Vit'a N'kanga or Antonio I), the famous war of Mbuila in 1665 would temporarily halt all hope of returning to the ancient order: This unfortunate history of the kingdom of Kongo marks the beginning of the reign of the eclipse mentioned by the myth of Nzala Mpânda.

The penetration of Black Africa by explorers from the West was first done in the Kingdom of Kongo in the 15th century. This penetration was not only the work of trading expeditions, but also of ecclesiastical armada which facilitated their task through evangelism. So it is through Kongo nation that Christianity penetrated first the soul of the Black African man.

Thus, the conclusions drawn there from the 15th century by missionaries became paradigms that will subsequently applied in Angola, Mozambique and throughout Black Africa. These paradigms, spread across Africa, the eclipse began at Kingdom of Kongo.

13.1 The eclipse at the Kingdom of Kongo

As I said above the stop over in Zimbabwe was a diversion intended to hide the great mystery at the heart of Africa, i.e., in the Congo Basin, as this high Spirituality is the key to the future return of the Nzala Mpânda. The decision to hide the great mystery was dictated by the prophecies which have been announced since Thoth up to Simon Kimbangu about the future struggle between light and darkness, between the lunar thought and solar thought.

It is this same logic that is asserted when Professor Margaret Washington explains, speaking of the first Portuguese expedition to Kongo: "The Portuguese explorers of the Order of Christ (a branch of Freemasonry) were in possession of a mirror through which they found most of the lands. So as the Magi discovered the birth of Christ by a star, it is also in the same way that the Portuguese explorers discovered the Kingdom of Kongo on which shone a very big star. "[89]

---

[89] Margaret, M., Le Legs universel de Kimpa Vita aux peuples

The veiled mission of the Portuguese navigator was it in really to come to stifle the circumstances that were to cause the third Nzala Mpânda? In any case the unfortunate events that followed the arrival of the Portuguese in the Kingdom of Kongo: destruction of the kingdom, slavery which deprived the kingdom of its valiant heads, malice, even the bestiality of the colonization of Congo and Angola, the tenacity of modern superpowers to Balkanize the Democratic Republic of Congo, etc., these events leave no shadow of doubt on the malicious intentions of the West vis-à-vis of a civilization of which they are aware of the formidable and imminent awakening.

The logical consequence of the eclipse, the struggle between the lunar thought and the solar thought is the abandonment by the Black man of his high spirituality and its epistemology and the influence exerted on him by the materiality of the Western system. The prophet Simon Kimbangu speaking of the paroxysm of this blindness among the Bakôngo said in his sermon in the forest of Mbanza Nsanda: "The progeny of Kongo will lose everything. It will be confused by the teachings and pervert moral principles of the European world (*mavânga ma Besimputu*). It will not anymore know the marital principles of its ancestors. It will ignore its mother tongue."[90]

---

noirs, http:/ /pbs.org/wgbh/aia/part1/1i3077.

[90] Kiatezua Lubanzadio Luyaluka, *la Religion kôngo*, Paris : l'Harmattan, 2010, p. 149.

It is important that Black Africans remember always that the eclipse has usually an ephemeral existence. The blinding materialism of the West has reached its peak. This materialism has developed in the Western society the seeds of its own destruction: rampant immorality, degradation of spiritual values, disastrous ethical positions that make of its science an insane instrument, etc.

The darkest night always precedes the dawn. The time has come for the Black of Africa and of the diaspora to prepare themselves for the end of their benightedness. It is time for us to begin our return to the solar epistemology that made our glory during the two Nzala Mpânda. It is time for us to start celebrating the beginning of the advent of solar thought in this third millennium.

14 THE NEXT NZALA MPÂNDA

The return of the Nzala Mpânda is a conviction that inhabits the heart of great Black-African initiates. Because they all know that finally Nzala Mpânda was not dead, he only eclipsed himself by going to the ancestors. It is thus from the sacred abode of the ancestors also that he will soon come back to mark humanity by his spiritual revelations which will bring the elevation of the Black-African civilization, and the return of his scientific community to the epistemological bases which made his former glory.

14.1 The destiny of fetishes

One cannot stick on that which is palliative and temporary and at the same time develop the summit of the true initiatory power which the divine mystery confers, the summit of the solar science and the technology which results from it. The great Kongo initiates were conscious of this truth; they were persuaded that the destiny of the fetishes is inscribed on the plan of their being abandoned, for an efficient preparation of the coming of the second Nzala Mpânda.

This conviction could be read in the action of the great spiritual figures of the Kongo nation who appeared since the start of the eclipse announced by the myth of Nzala Mpânda: apolonia Mafuta, Kimpa Vita, Simon Kimbangu, etc. All these Kongo prophets worked to convince their brothers of race about the need to abandon the fetishes and witchcraft, two great shackles against the exercise of the power conferred by the divine mystery.

14.2 The imminence of the next Nzala Mpânda

The imminence of the next Nzala Mpânda can be inferred from the fact that the "night" of the Mvumbi Mbumbulu is the product of an ephemeral phenomenon, a phenomenon that lasts only a fraction of the length of a day.

Of all the initiates of our time, Simon Kimbangu is the more explicit with respect to the conviction of the imminent arrival of the Nzala Mpânda. While there was no indication, he yet predicted the end of colonization in Africa, the Kongo prophet announced in i921 that the

Whites will go; leaving Africa in the hands of Black leaders, who unfortunately at the beginning will all work for the benefit of the West.

Simon Kimbangu did not stop at the affirmation of the certainty of the independence of African nations, but he also predicted the imminent coming of the supremacy of the solar thought the advent of the Nzala Mpânda, in words that revolted the colonial power of Belgium-Congo: "The Black man will become White and the White man will become Black."[91]

In the interpretation of this prophecy, modern disciples of the great Kongo prophet are unanimous: it will not be a transmutation of race, but rather an epistemological shift that will mark the end of the eclipse mentioned by the myth of Nzala Mpanda. This eclipse is none other than the brand of the current Black-African society mired in empirical-materialistic rationalism that does not fit at all with our deepest identity. That the Black man will become White implies thus, in their mutual relations, the transfer of the superpower will start to happen soon from the Western to the African!

15 CONCLUSION

A wise man once said to a young Congolese artist that myths are facts that by being often told became transformed. One of the Kongo myths that until now remained a headache for any attempt of hermeneutics

---

[91] Kiatezua Lubanzadio Luyaluka, *la Religion kôngo*, Paris : l'Harmattan, 2010, p. 147.

is the myth of Nzala Mpânda; this myth has thus remained unexplained by tradition as well as by anthropologists and naturalists.

In this book, thanks to an ethno-linguistic analysis, I gave readers an interpretation of this myth that shows that it is a profound teaching left to Black Africans of today by their ancestors to help them understand the origins and destiny of fetishes in their culture.

This myth shows the Black African man that originally fetishes, or human *min'kisi* are a means used by African initiates of the divine mystery for the transmission of their power by simple faith in matter and in the ancetors, as a palliative and temporary power to be used in their absence.

This myth tells us that the Black-African civilization has known in the past two golden ages when, thanks to the high spirituality, Black African science has raised its technology at the highest point; the Black man arrived at this feat based on solar epistemology, a philosophical approach that is appropriate to him.

Based on this interpretation and assumption of an Egyptian origin the Bantu, I supported the hypothesis that the first peak of the solar thinking took place in Egypt; it was followed by the exodus to the Bantu to Central Africa, considered by the ancient Egyptians as their "holy land." This exodus was also that of the Egyptian great mystery.

The second peak of the Black-African civilization which is alluded in this myth took place in Zimbabwe. It is at the end of this second peak that fetishes will be introduced by the Bantu initiates in their system, because they were well aware of the prophecies concerning the future hibernation of their civilization; hibernation during which the lunar Western thought, would dominate for a time the solar thought.

The myth of Nzala Mpânda teaches us that the reign of the lunar thought is ephemeral, and that the Black African man should prepare himself for the imminent epistemological shift that will bring the supremacy of his civilization on the scientific and technological level. And in the perspective of this advent, the destiny of the fetishes is in the necessity of their abandonment for the high spirituality that made the glory of Black-African civilization in Egypt and in Zimbabwe.

16 REFERENCES

1. Bahelele Ndimisa, *Lusansu ye fu bien nkongo*, Kinshasa : CEDI, 1977.
2. Batshikama ba Mampuya ma Ndwala, R., *Voici les Jagas*, Kinshasa, 1971.
3. Bentley, H., *Dictionary and grammar of the kôngo language*.
4. Cheik Anta Diop, *Antériorité des civilisations nègres*, Présence africaine, Abidjan, 1972.
5. Dumont, J., *L'histoire générale de l'Afrique*, Paris, 1972.
6. Dumont, J., *L'histoire générale de l'Afrique*, Paris, 1972.
7. Fukiau, A., *le Mukongo et le monde qui l'entourait*, Kinshasa, 1969.
8. Hérodote, *An account of Egypt*, www.gutenberg.org.
9. Janzen : *Lemba, 1650-1930*, New York : Garland Publishing inc.
10. Kimfoko Madoungou, J., *le Guide du musée*, Pointe-Noire, 1985.
11. Kimpianga Mahaniah, *la Problématique crocodilienne à Luozi*, Kinshasa, 1989.
12. Laman, K., *Dictionnaire kikongo-français*.
13. Lusala lu Ne Nkuka, « les Traces de dieu dans les cultures » in *Congo nova*, http://www.congonova.org.
14. Mackenzie, D., *Egyptian Myth and Legend*, www.sacred-texts.com.
15. Maspero, *History of Egypt Chaldea, Syria, Babylonia, and Assyria*, www.gutenberg.org.
16. Massey, *Ancient Egypt the light of the world*, www.masseiana.org.

17. Massey, *Book of the begining*, www.masseiana.org.
18. Mvog Ekang, *Cameroun – religion traditionnelle*, www.facebook.com/topic.php?uid=329561433865&topic=15405.
19. Pierre, N., *Moïse, l'Africain*, Paris. Menaibuc 2001
20. Rawlinson, G., *Ancient Egypt*, www.gutenberg.org.
21. Schuré, E., *les Grands initiés*, Perrin, Paris, 1970.
22. Van Wing, J., *Etudes Bakôngo*, Léopoldville, 1938.
23. Washington, M., *Le Legs universel de Kimpa Vita aux peuples noirs*, http /pbs.org/wgbh/aia/part1/1i3077.
24. Webster, H., *la Magie dans les sociétés primitives*, Paris : Payot, 1952.

WHAT IS THE INSTITUT DES SCIENCES ANIMIQUES

The Institut des Sciences Animiques (ISA) is a center of reserch in afrocentric spirituatlity and philosophy created by Dr Kiatezua L. Luyaluka (Ph.D. (Honours) in Theology). The Iainms at the understanding of:

- The true and the highest adrocentric spirituality, its Egyptian origins and its convergence with Christianity.

- The necessity and the pertinence of the afrocentric epistemology for the scientific, technological, cultural and political progress of the Black man.

- The efficiency of the fight against witchcraft.

Dr Kiatezua shares his experience of divine metaphysics accumulated since 34 years by organizing seminars on spirituality and the fight against witchcraft. To learn more about ISA go to our blog:

www.animic.wordpress.com

To contact us :

E-mail: isa.ongd@yahoo.fr
Tél. : 00243999935562
00242053214614

TO BE READ: **KEMETIC THOUGHT**

Quarterly journal of afrocentric spirituality, **Kemetic Thoughs** presents Black-African religion by exposing its high theology and its practical import. This journal of ISA shows also to the Black-African man the necessity of an epistemological revolution which must bring the supremacy of the solar thinking over the lunar thinking of the West